A butterfly on my wine glass

To Kizzy,

With much love,

Annie.

xp

A butterfly on my wine glass

Travel guide to Nouvelle-Aquitaine:
the Gironde and Dordogne areas of SW France

Annie Jefferies

Illustrations by
Louise Wakeford

YouCaxton Publications
Oxford & Shrewsbury

ISBN 978-1-913425-34-0

Published by YouCaxton Publications 2020

YCBN: 01

Illustrations ©Louise Wakeford

YouCaxton Publications

enquiries@youcaxton.co.uk

Contents

This book is dedicated to my three beautiful nieces
Emily, Laura and Lucy for their love and inspiration.

Preface

It is often difficult to pin-point exact events in one's life, other than major events such as the assassination of John Kennedy and the death of Diana, Princess of Wales. For instance when did I actually fall so much in love with France? The seeds were definitely sown when I was 16 years old and I had a pen friend who lived in Lyon, but whose family skied in St Gervais in the French Alps during the winter months. Jeanne and her family invited me to St Gervais for Christmas and New Year in 1965. I was a little tentative about the whole trip, especially as I flew from Lydd Airport in Kent to Lyon on one of those planes where the cockpit was a part of the main cabin, and the air hostess served everything from a crate at the back of the plane. The engine noise was so loud that you couldn't actually hear any of the announcements and I was far too young to even consider having a large gin and tonic to calm my nerves. In those days I was just about being introduced to a very occasional Babycham!

However I should never have worried about being away from home at Christmas. Jeanne's family were wonderfully kind and welcoming and as we drove in *Monsieur's* Citroen up to the French Alps, I delighted in the mountainous landscape, cows with bells and all of the alpine villages traditionally decorated for Christmas, although at this point there was no sign of a single snowflake. On Christmas Eve we dutifully went to midnight mass; I am not a Catholic but I loved the whole atmosphere of the service from the vast amounts of incense been swung around, to the bells ringing with great joy and vigour to welcome in Christmas morning, and as we came out of Church at 1am, joy of joys it was snowing so heavily that in the morning all of the pavements had disappeared, and the vast mountainside was covered in a huge blanket of snow. The whole holiday was magical and my love affair with France definitely began on that visit.

Although I had several visits to different areas of France in the next few years either on family holidays or school trips, the next event that strongly influenced me occurred when I was 24 years and one of my younger sisters, who was 19 years at the time, went to live in Geneva. During the next ten years I spent many a holiday with Louise, and as she eventually married and had her children, I had the added pleasure of getting to know my niece and nephews in their own environments. Although Geneva is in Switzerland, it is on the French border, predominately the local language is French. In the winter in the Alps cheese *fondue* and *raclette* are favourite meals, in the summer *filets des perches* at the restaurants on Lake Geneva were so tasty and for me all of my visits only enhanced my delight in all things French!

As the years have gone by my husband, Mike, and I have spent a lot of time in Europe in our Motorhome, mostly in France, Spain and Italy, so when it was my 70th birthday last August, the obvious choice of place to spend it was in France. My sister had now retired and the family live in Pellegrue, a village almost halfway between Bergerac and Bordeaux, and she had suggested that we rent a house in the Gironde region for a period of time over the summer. What a perfect idea and we found a lovely house in the grounds of a chateau.

However things never go to plan and earlier in the year I had had a fall into a mains drain, and in order to prevent any infection within the 16 stitch thigh wound, I had been prescribed two concurrent courses of an antibiotic to which it turned out I was very allergic. By the end of June, I had drug-induced jaundice and hepatitis. The Hepatology medical team eventually, and somewhat reluctantly, agreed that I could leave the country, but I had strict instructions to go to the local hospital in France for regular blood tests and not a drop of alcohol was to pass my lips for the foreseeable future, certainly not until I attended the Liver Unit again in England in September.

I should perhaps now add, that the house we were renting was smack bang in the middle of a vineyard, and all of our guests who were coming to stay were great wine enthusiasts who wanted to tour and taste, as many different local wines as was feasibly possible; several were travelling down to SW France by car with the very intention of buying several cases of wine to take home, so this was indeed a serious business and Mike was already busy planning the *dégustation* schedule!

I realised within a couple of days of arriving that there was no point whatsoever in me joining what sounded to be like endless wine tasting sessions, but luckily I had my own car, our Labrador dog , my sister living within 10 miles and the swimming pool! Also of course I was feeding up to 12 guests at a time so there were always meals to plan and prepare, although the men took over much of it with BBQs, especially in the evening when we sat in candlelight by the pool and how handy are the French *patisseries* for wonderful desserts?

Then in the middle of the night it came to me, I had always wanted to write; poetry was not my thing, an autobiography might be difficult without upsetting the whole family and most of our friends, a novel would probably need lots of imagination, but the idea had struck a chord and I decided that "writing" would be my summer project!

Introduction
Planting the seeds of authorship

Well here goes …

I have always done a vast amount of report writing in my career, but a book felt very different. However the principles did seem to be much the same, lots of research, a clear plan regarding the layout and if I ever got that far, a reputable proof reader and publisher.

Once I thought about it as a definite project, it wasn't difficult to decide what theme to focus on. I had spent the first week attempting to buy a decent guide book on the local area and although there were plenty of books on the area north of the Dordogne River, around Bergerac, Sarlat and Rocmadour etc, I could find very little on the Gironde department south of the Dordogne River in Nouvelle-Aquitaine. A trip to the English bookshop in Bordeaux confirmed that, apart from Bordeaux itself, there was indeed a dearth of books on local points of interest in this particular region of the Gironde and yet as I explored the local villages and towns I found there was masses to discover.

The Gironde is a department in the Nouvelle-Aquitaine region of South West France. It is named after the Gironde estuary and, most notably, the Bordeaux Wine region is in the Gironde. It is surrounded by the departments of Landes, Dordogne, Lot-et-Garonne, Charente-Maritime and the Atlantic Ocean on the west. Entre-Deux-Mers is a wine region in Bordeaux, situated between the rivers Garonne and the Dordogne and is bounded in the east by the Gironde department. This is the largest sub region of Bordeaux. The Bordeaux region is naturally divided into a left bank area, which includes the Medoc and Graves and a right bank which includes the Libournais, Bourg and Blaye. Apart from Entre-Deux-Mers, there are also the Libournais sub regions of St Emilion and Pomerol, smaller in hectares than Entre-Deux-Mers, but much more prolific in their wine production.

All of these regions (except the Libournais) have their own *appellation* and are governed by *appellation d'origin contrõllée* laws which dictate the permissible grape varieties and wine making techniques. However this book is not intended as a guide to wine making, a complex subject that has formed the basis of many distinguished books. The description above is meant to give an idea of the geographical boundaries of the area, which inevitably are linked to the wine growing boundaries.

This book is primarily intended as an anecdotal guide to accompany visitors on their discovery of this attractive but perhaps less well known area of SW France. I hope you will enjoy reading it.

Annie Jefferies

CHAPTER 1:
First impressions

We had rented a delightful old French property for the months of July and August 2019 which had been renovated some 10 years ago from what was apparently a run-down barn. The renovation had been done sensitively and very tastefully, with the intention of appealing to both families and adult groups. The house was situated on the outskirts of the hamlet of St-Andre-et Appelles, two miles from Sainte-Foy-la-Grande, located in the grounds of a chateau, surrounded by vineyards and wonderful views over the valley. The house was spacious and well equipped with six double bedrooms, all with en-suite bathrooms. The swimming pool was a bonus, as were the 12 comfortable loungers and umbrellas surrounding the pool area and the BBQ area.

So Mike, Harry (our 4 year old Labrador) and I were happily settled in and awaiting the first of our summer visitors. Mike was busy planning wine tasting trips to the various local *caves,* of which there were an abundance and I was starting to consider the research I needed for my book.

In my new found state of enforced sobriety I was eager to start searching the area for interesting places to visit. Markets were the first obvious places to start, and became places where I could have a coffee and a look at the stalls with our visitors, before they went off wine tasting while I spent an hour or two with Harry, walking through the cobbled streets in the balmy heat of a summer day. This was a wonderful way to do my research as we came across interesting art galleries, craft studios and book shops. I found people were very willing to converse with me despite my sometimes limited language skills. Harry too, was a useful companion for his presence often gave me the introductory conversation, as shopkeepers and artisans would invite him into the cool of their building, ask his name and age and usually offer him a bowl of water. Then followed a discussion on their livelihood which in most instances I found to be fascinating and very educational! I actually decided this was much more fun than being with the rest of our friends undertaking yet another "*dégustation*"…After a few weeks I began to feel like a real native of this beautiful area.

Markets in France

The traditional markets are an important part of the French way of life. The market as a source of fresh fruit and vegetables demonstrates the French people's commitment to cooking and healthy eating, including well stocked fish counters and excellent meat "cuts" which warrant the queues that develop as the morning progresses. The cheese stalls give the most mouth-watering aroma and have a substantial selection of different cheeses. Most markets have expanded over the years to include a comprehensive range of traders, ensuring that a "whole shopping experience" is available in a couple of hours. Clothes stalls with brightly coloured dresses, shorts, trousers and sun tops offer an enticing variety of styles, colours and sizes. A mock changing room is often set up in the clothes van, which when the door is shut is so dark, that you can't actually view the garment in the mirror, resulting in most people trying on their proposed purchases at the back of the stall with suitable advice given from the accompanying friend or stall holder. Sun hats, shoes, flip flops, sun shades, linen tablecloths and the traditional plastic variety are on display, and long rolls of fabric are immediately cut to the desired length. Pottery, wood turned items and wicker baskets all have pride of place on their individual stalls, as do belts, scarves and haberdashery. Many markets have a wide range of artisan items, which demonstrate the skills of local artists and craft workers.

Most towns and larger villages have a weekly market, although in larger towns markets may take place twice a week or even daily. The market opens at 7.30am and usually closes at 1pm, although in the summer many towns have markets which open in the evening, when the atmosphere is more of a "fair", with music playing whilst families come and buy a variety of delicious dishes to consume, accompanied by bottles of local wine. As the evening progresses dancing will begin and the whole atmosphere is one of a huge party.

The morning markets are indeed also places for people to meet up, shop and then have coffee together. Most markets are surrounded by patisseries and cafe/restaurants for people to stop and have a light lunch as midday arrives. Others will just enjoy sitting at the pavement cafes, sampling a glass of the local wine or a chilled beer.

These markets quickly became a favourite of mine, especially as there was fresh produce to buy almost on a daily basis to feed a houseful of hungry people. The only requirement is to know which market is in which town or village on which day!

Market days in Gironde around the wider area of Sainte-Foy-la-Grande

Monday	- Duras
Tuesday	- Sauveterre
Wednesday	- Pellegrue
Thursday	- Eymet
Friday	- Monsegur
Saturday	- Ste Foy la Grande
Sunday	- Issegeac, (plus market stalls selling *brocante and antiquitiés*)

There are large supermarkets too in the area: one particular chain appears on the edge of all reasonably sized towns and sells anything one might require, from equipping a house with white electrical goods, to sports and gardening equipment. It is often possible to find a hairdressers in situ, a pharmacy, plus a large *magasin de la presse,* one of the few places in this area of France where you can usually buy an English newspaper!

The whole area is a mass of **vineyards** as far as the eye can see and it is quite permissible to walk through vineyards even for dog walking. This is very useful as there is hardly a scrap of land in the vast department that isn't devoted to grape production. As a result the land looks lush and colourful as the vineyards, with their green and purple grapes, are often interspersed with fields of huge sunflowers. The sunflowers are wonderful, very tall and with all of the "faces" turned towards the sun. The whole countryside looks very open and because there are no hedges dividing fields, the areas of visible land seem vast.

Un beau tournesol

Almost all of the Chateaux welcome visitors for wine tasting, *dégustation*, although there is an unsaid expectation that visitors will at least be tempted to buy some bottles of the wines that have been tasted and enjoyed.

Churches

Churches feature in every village and town and often have exposed bell towers which are interesting as different shaped towers abound the area. The churchyards too are lovely to visit as the memorial stones are well cared for, mostly decorated with a range of silk flowers, photographs of deceased relatives in attractive frames and often ceramic carvings contain poems and readings favoured by the family. France is of course a Catholic country and although the priests are very welcoming to visitors attending church services, it is very much frowned upon if an Anglican attempts to receive Holy Communion at a Catholic Mass.

Roads

The roads are a delight to drive along, mostly straight and often with little traffic. Compared to being on the over populated roads in the UK, the quietness of these roads really enhances the enjoyment of travelling from place to place. The signposts are clear and it is easy to acclimatise oneself to the geography of an area. The main danger on the road are the cyclists! The French love cycling and because the roads are very flat, it is an appropriate way of staying fit. In the summer it is easy to hire bikes and there are many companies who will take luggage on ahead to the agreed accommodation, hence it is a very popular holiday for families with younger children.

Cafes and restaurants

These are prolific and although standards will clearly vary in the main the food is very reasonably priced and of a good quality. At lunchtime by law all restaurants in France will offer a *plat du jour* at a set price; this will always include a starter and a main course, usually a dessert and occasionally a glass of wine to accompany the meal. It is usually much better value than eating out in the same restaurant in the evening. Local wines are sold by the glass or in a carafe, as well as by the bottle. House wines are always good quality and much cheaper. Beer is often sold by the bottle although *bière a la pression* refers to draft beer or lager. The real ales that many men drink in England are not available, and the term "beer" usually relate to lagers and much lighter ales.

CHAPTER 2:
Enjoying the countryside

The countryside is a delight. Due to the climate the area is very green and lush and has a soporific gentleness about it. The houses are built of mellow sandstone, most have shutters which are painted soothing colours and the gardens are full of scented flowers: roses, lavender and many variety of herbs that give a wonderful aroma in the warm summer air. There are many blossoming fruit trees and lime trees which not only are attractive to look at, but also give shade to pedestrians and customers outside pavement cafes. Many villages are awarded with the accolade *village fleurie* and for good reason. Colourful geraniums, begonias, petunias, fuschias and lobelia trail from hanging baskets on street lights and from window boxes attached to houses in the streets. Then there are the large tubs of plants that are dotted between trees lining the pavement; the whole effect is of enhancing ones overall sense of well-being and pleasure.

Most villages have a lake or river in its vicinity. Being so near to large rivers such as the Dordogne, the Garonne, the Lot and others that is not surprising; it is however very helpful when it is a hot summers' day and you have a young black Labrador who is longing for a swim…dogs are never allowed in swimming pools but a nearby lake serves an excellent solution for cooling off after a walk. Driving around the countryside one spots many areas for picnics and in this area of France, there are often artificially sanded sites referred to as *la plage*. These areas are specifically for families and those who want to sunbathe, picnic, take a boat on the lake, play volleyball or enjoy a more sedate game of *pétanque*.

One of the interesting sights in the countryside in this area are the **tobacco drying sheds.** During the past 150 years the Dordogne area enjoyed real wealth from tobacco growing. It was a hugely important industry that created a lot of prosperity and indeed work in the region. The tobacco plant itself was large, robust and ideally suited to small farms, like many of those in the Gironde and Dordogne regions. Tobacco had a high and stable value, was happy to grow in low fertile soils and was less perishable and easier to store than most alternative crops. Once a familiar sight, the industry has now collapsed. A change of ownership of Gauloise and Gitaines cigarette brands sent the growing of the tobacco to Spain, home of the new owners. Until 2012, there was a modest subsidy to keep some tobacco growing in France, but with smoking officially discouraged government subsidy was hardly supportable.

Grange de séchage de tabac

Bergerac was the production site for the cigarettes. The local farmers grew, harvested and dried the tobacco for the factory. Traditional air-drying barns were built in stone and wood, with covered roofs but opening sides that channel air circulation over the hanging leaves. It takes about four to eight weeks to complete the drying process. Surprisingly it is an exacting business: drying too quickly and the leaves will dry patchily, too slowly and they begin to rot. Sadly the surrounding region now has hundreds of empty tobacco drying sheds, dotted around the countryside, many are now used simply as barns, some converted to holiday *gites*, whilst others are just left derelict.

Gardens

On one of my regular jaunts around the countryside I came across **Les Jardins de Sardy.** These *jardins* are situated in Velines and directions can be found via their website **www.jardindesardy.com**. The foundations of Sardy date back to the middle ages when Sardy was a fortified farm. The winery and the dovecote in the courtyard were built around 1650, while the main house and the long pool were built around 1740. The present garden is designed around the long pool and is the work of Betty and Bertie Imbs, with contributions from an architect, Louis Aublet, and a garden designer, Jacques Desmartis. The gardens are not large but have an appearance of Italy with rising cypress trees, combined with the romantic charm of many English gardens with a rock garden and mixed borders. The gardens are framed at the end of the rock pool by the shuttered windows of a typically French house which adds to the calmness and ambience of the gardens. It was in these gardens that I saw my first butterflies in France, *les papillons* sounds such a descriptive name as these beautiful creatures are so delicate and have the appearance of being paper thin. There were several coloured varieties that day floating gently in the air above the lake, landing on the aromatic flowers and shrubs before drifting off to leafy twig that caught their attention.

Typically after any visits such as this I found an inviting stone staircase signposted to the *Salon de thé* for a refreshing drink and patisserie, whilst sitting on a shaded terrace enjoying the scents from the courtyard climbing roses.

Walking and Cycling

Walking and cycling are pursuits much enjoyed in this region of France. The area is relatively flat for cycling, the roads are quiet and the towns all have bike hire shops. Walking is a very popular as you can walk anywhere and the *vignerons* do not mind if you walk through the rows of vines. There are signed walking routes particularly through forested areas, but in the main the countryside is so open that it is very straightforward to follow any route you choose to take. In France the vineyards are planted on open areas of lands which makes walking through this glorious countryside a pure delight. This is very unlike England where fields are separated by hedges, gates and stiles.

The Pilgrims Way

The Pilgrim's Way (Camino Way) heading towards Santiago de Compostela has many routes in this SW area of France. The famous scallop shells found embedded in the cobble streets or in the stone work of walls, direct people towards the Pyrenees and on into Spain. Many people wear the scallop shells around their neck as they walk to ensure safety and good luck along the route. In this area the Voie de Vezelay is the traditional route that enters the South Gironde at Ste-Foy-la-Grande and passes through the Entre-Deux-Mers vineyards for over a hundred kilometres, until it enters the Landes de Gascogne forest, Along the route pilgrim hostels provide good basic overnight accommodation and often with a communal evening meal.

La coquille Saint Jaques de Compostelle

Canoeing

Canoing is a popular sport in this region and it is easy to find kayaking and canoe outlets in towns along the key rivers, such as the Dordogne. There is a canoe base at Ste-Foy-la-Grande, but during the summer when we were in residence, the water levels were very low and the only way to do some decent kayaking was to travel upstream, by car, to Sarlat or Rocamadour. Both places are two to three hours away by car but the scenery *en route* makes the trip really enjoyable.

Golf

Golf is not so commonplace, although there were several nine hole courses in the region. The main and most popular golf course is at Vigiers, which has three nine hole courses, a combination of whichever course makes up the 18 holes of this beautifully manicured establishment. There is a much smaller course at St-Meard-de-Gurcon and a private members course at St Emilion. At any of these golf courses it is perfectly permissible to pop in for coffee or lunch on their terraces overlooking the courses.

Back at our home in St-Andre-et-Appelles we realise what wonderful walks there are around our own property. Apart from the grape vines, we discover walnut and plum trees and other fruit trees in abundance and quite surprisingly blackthorn bushes full of sloe berries. The blackthorn bushes are densely packed and full of thorns, as they are grown to keep livestock in check. Sloes are a member of the prunus family and the bushes are covered in white blossom in the spring. When picking these rather attractive looking berries, do not be tempted to taste one as they are very bitter; however soaking the sloes in gin makes a splendid Christmas drink! Our landlady had never made Sloe Gin, so this was our chance to introduce her to the delicious liquor

Sloe Gin recipe
Requirements;
500g / 1lb of sloes
250g / 8ozs of sugar
70cl Gin
A demijohn or similar airtight jar that holds 1.5 litres

Method

Pick out the sloes to remove any stems and put them in the freezer overnight or for as long as you want. The reason for putting the sloes in the freezer is that it removes the need for the sloes to be pricked individually with a fork, to release the juices. Once out of the freezer put the sloes in the clean airtight jar, add the sugar and cover the sloes and sugar with the bottle of gin. Repeat the process with the same quantities again. Keep the empty gin bottles for the finished sloe liquor.

Give the jar or demijohn a good shake to start the sugar dissolving and store in a cool darkened cupboard. Every week bring the jar out and give it a shake. Repeat this process until all of the sugar has dissolved and then leave the jar in the dark cupboard for up to three months. At this point strain the mixture, which should be a rich plum colour, through a muslin cloth using a funnel back into the original gin bottles and sample! The old sloes can now be discarded.

To make a Sloe Spritz:

Although the gin is lovely on its own, or drizzled as a liquor over a dessert or a cake, it can also be used as an *apéritif or digestif.*

Simply pour 25ml of the sloe gin into a champagne glass and add prosecco. Add ice as desired and a slice of orange or lemon.

Santé

CHAPTER 3:
Exploring Bastide Villages

Bastide villages are defined as fortified villages or towns in France, usually built in Languedoc, Gascony and Aquitaine mainly in the 13th and 14th centuries. Some of the first *bastides* were built under Raymond VII of Toulouse to replace villages destroyed in the Albigensian Crusade. He encouraged the construction of others in south west France where there were vast regions of "wilderness" with small populations. Almost 700 *bastide* villages were built between 1222 and 1372.

The *bastides* were so successful against their opponents in the Hundred Years War, that the English adopted them for themselves in France and later in Wales. As the *bastide* villages grew, the new inhabitants were encouraged to cultivate the surrounding land and to attract trade in the form of merchants and markets. The *bastide* central square usually had a covered hall and church which were originally constructed of wood, although these were later replaced by stone structures.

panneau bastide

Each *Bastide* village is identified by a tourist sign at the entrance to the village: a brown sign with a square of squares, with the central one missing. Many *bastide* villages have survived the passing of time, with some being beautifully restored such as Eymet, Montpelier, Montflauquin, Domme, Rudelle and Villefranche du Perigord.

Pellegrue:

This is a small Bastide village with lots of interesting features. The population is only just over a thousand. The houses in the village are traditional stone houses that lead from the War Memorial to the Eglise Saint-Andre, a 12th century Romanesque church. In the course of the development of the church square, archaeologists found remains of a Gallo-Roman settlement, with monolithic limestone sarcophagi and graves from the 11th century. They also discovered walls of a Benedictine priory and part of a medieval castle. Nearby to the church is a modern fountain, Font de Godemine which is located in an ancient square. Pellegrue has a large 19th century iron market hall which is surrounded by traditional covered arcades. Market day is on Wednesday.

Halle de bastide

There are two particularly interesting facts about Pellegrue. One is the name which derives from the *Grue,* and *pella grua* means a flock of *grues.* A *grue* is a common crane which inhabits this area of SW France in the summer months. In October the massive birds fly away en masse to migrate. The noise of their departure is deafening as the birds herald their *au revoirs* to the local residents with an incessant krou-krou-krou noise. Cranes are a part of the Gruidae family, they are one of the largest birds in Europe with a wingspan of two meters and a weight of between four and six lbs.

The second interesting fact about Pellegrue is the brass replicas of the shell of St James, referred to and illustrated in the previous chapter, which one can spot embedded in the cobbles of the streets, as an indication that this village is on one of the pilgrim routes from France to Santiago de Compostela i.e. The Camino Way. This pilgrim route follows the GR654 (west) via Lemovicensis to Camino de Santiago.

Another unexpected find in Pellegrue was the studio of local artist **Claire Scofield**, a talented French lady who exhibits in local towns throughout the summer months. There is more about Claire in Chapter 10 on Arts and Crafts.

Monsegur

Monsegur is another attractive *bastide* village in Gironde about 46 miles from Bordeaux, but only 10 miles from Pellegrue. The village was founded by Eleanor of Aquitaine in 1265, and its name means "hill of safety". The layout follows a classic *bastide* design, with a village square surrounded by arches, off which run narrow streets. The village hosts a busy market alongside a range of festivals throughout the year. The most famous and very popular annual event is the 24 Hours of Swing de Monsegur. This jazz festival lasts for 3 days in July and draws all age groups from all over France. The opening ceremony for the jazz festival is a musical parade through the village streets.

Monpazier:

Montpazier is a large village in the Dordogne department in Nouvelle-Aquitaine. The village is a member of the most beautiful villages in France association. It is a 13th century *bastide* village and was home to Eleanor of Aquitaine and Richard II of England for a time. It is acknowledged as a model *bastide* based on its perfect layout. The market is held on a Thursday morning, but apart from the market stall holders, the village is home to many artists and crafts people. The village features a Bastideum which takes you through the history of *bastides,* covering the architecture and heritage of the villages through the middle ages. Underneath the arches surrounding the market square there are a selection of shops containing artisan products and souvenirs and, of course, cafes. An attractive village that offers an enjoyable visit.

Eymet

Eymet is a large village in the Dordogne department in Nouvelle-Aquitaine. It is popular with British expatriates who account for about a third of the local population of between two to three thousand. The village is worth a visit as it is one of the few *bastides* to still have a fortified castle, with the walls and dungeons still standing. The Eymet *bastide* was created in 1270 by Alphonse, Count of Poitiers and also Toulouse. Today Eymet is a bustling hub offering a range of activities, including an evening market, an Oyster and Wine Festival and Medieval Roaming in the Dropt Valley. Because of the higher number of British residing in and around Eymet, there is a wide cultural diversity and apart from the usual facilities found in a French village, there is also a cricket ground which hosts games between the local French and English residents. Although it is a pretty village to visit, I found the occasional group of expatriates huddled together in cafes and shopping using only English to purchase their products from the market stall holders a little disappointing.

Rendez-vous aux marchés !

All of the villages have their own tourist offices, which are always well stocked with leaflets on local musical events, art exhibitions and maps of the area. Sadly missing are the guide books in English on the local history and places of interest to visit. Quite a few of our guests had limited French and would have appreciated an English version to take with them on the days they went out in the car to explore.

CHAPTER 4:
Duras and Issegeac

Duras and Issegeac are interesting villages to visit

Duras

Duras is a delightful village some 10 miles south from Ste-Foy-la-Grande. It is attractively positioned on top of a hill due to the fortification requirements of the castle. Market day is on Monday, when the square and adjoining streets are full of colourful stalls and cheery stallholders. Not only are the usual fruit and vegetable stalls selling their wonderful local produce, but flower stalls too entice buyers, although I personally feel that flowers are relatively expensive to buy in France compared to the low-priced bunches of daffodils and sweet peas that we can buy in Devon. However the scent is wonderful as you linger at the flower stalls, and it is after all attractive and very French, to have a bunch of local flowers on the kitchen table when you are eating bread and cheese, cold meats or pates, salads and fresh fruit washed down with a chilled local wine!

I love the traditional woven shopping baskets that every French woman carries to the market, so I had to be very circumspect in reminding myself that there are only so many baskets you need, or indeed can carry! At the Duras market I purchased an amazingly long table cloth with 12 matching linen napkins for 45 euros which I felt was really good value and is much admired at home. The pottery is lovely, as are the soaps, leather goods, scarves, linens, sun hats, carpets, etc.

Many of the stall holders move from one village market to another, so if there is a question about a sun dress size or a different coloured article, it can usually be obtained from the same stall holder at another market in the vicinity. If you are a " salesman's dream " type of person, as my husband frequently describes me, then the markets are a useful way of stocking up with birthday presents for family and friends, there is just so much choice ! After pottering around the market for an hour or so, it is definitely time for a *grande crème* coffee, in one of the delightful pavement cafes or the tapas bar before building up strength to visit the castle.

A visit to the **Chateau du Duras** is enjoyable, interesting and good value. Tickets for the visit can be purchased in the well-stocked gift shop.

The Chateau was first built in the 1100's, although redone in 1310 by Bertrand de Goth, nephew of Pope Clement V of Avignon. His niece married a member of the Dufort family and from 1325 the Chateau belonged to a powerful pro English family. In 1389 it was besieged by du Guesclin, but this did not stop the Duras-Duforts from returning and rebuilding the chateau that stands today. At the beginning of the 16th century, the Duras-Dufort family embraced the protestant faith and this was the beginning of their social ascension to become counts, marquis, dukes and eventually peers of France. In 1795 Louise Felicite Victoire d'Aumont became Princess Louise of Monaco when she married Prince Honore IV of Monaco. Prince Albert 11 of Monaco honoured Duras with a visit in July 2107 as Duras Castle is one of the historical sites of Monaco. The village purchased the Chateau in 1969 and undertook a 20 year restoration programme, which brought the Chateau back to life for modern day visitors to appreciate, not only for its architecture, but also the history of life at the Chateau with troubadours, knights, ladies and music. During the summer months *son et lumiere* productions are held twice weekly in the evening, tickets can be purchased at the Chateau or on line for these shows. Dinner on the terrace of a local restaurant followed by an enjoyable hour in the balmy air of a summer evening is a relaxing way to end a day in this village.

It would be remiss not to mention the writer Marguerite Donnadieu, a 20th century writer, who chose as her pen name **Marguerite Duras.** She is internationally known as an author, scriptwriter and film director; she is most famous as a major author in modern literature and recognised for her strong stances and the impact of her work on the literary world. After her death in 1977 a local society in the Lot-et-Garonne was created in her honour, which every year organises a small festival entitled *"Journées Marguerite Duras"*

Another author associated with Duras was **Claire de Kersaint** who as Duchess of Duras in the 19th century was one of the most likeable personalities of this period. She wrote several books, the most famous being "Ourika" which deals with race and gender issues.

Issegeac:

Issegeac is a wonderful old circular-shaped medieval village with masses of interesting features. It was built in the ages from the 13th -16th centuries, although many of the original buildings were erected much earlier with their roots founded in antiquity. It a very quaint village with timbered houses around the Church and the Bishops' Palace. Apart from the weekly, bustling Sunday market which is packed with people during the summer months, throughout the year the village hosts numerous festivals and events.

The thriving Sunday market not only has a wonderful array of local vegetable and fruit produce, meats, cheeses and fish, but there is also a large *antiquities* market to browse. The cafes dotted around the village are understandably crowded, with seats much sought after, as people travel from local towns and villages simply to enjoy the ambience of this colourful village. On the

Sundays that we visited Issegeac there were regular musicians who entertained the shoppers with accordion, cello, violin and saxophone playing. It is certainly a place to spend a few hours relaxing and absorbing the atmosphere of typical rural France.

L'entre deux mers - entre Garonne et Dordogne

CHAPTER 5:
Chateaux and Abbeys

There are an abundance of chateaux in the Gironde region of France, not surprisingly when the whole region is given over to vineyards and the production of superb wines. However as the word *chateau* equates to the English word for castle, there are some chateaux that one can visit in the traditional sense of the word to tour the medieval building.

Chateau de Monbazillac:

This famous chateau has been recognised as a national historical monument since the 16th century. Montbazillac is located a short distance from Bergerac and is set in the heart of the famous vineyard of the same name. The impressive chateau stands overlooking the Dordogne Valley with large garden terraces which visitors can enjoy. The chateau is modelled on an early Renaissance style, and built in 1550, it has remained intact through various wars and revolutions. It looks at first sight a little like a "Cinderella fairy tale castle", with its rounded turrets and pointed roofs. Inside there are three floors of the chateau to view; with large, light and leaded windows the rooms have an appearance of space and airiness. There is a small basement museum which houses the chateau's kitchen implements and wine making tools. The chateau in itself makes for a very interesting visit, but it is the locally produced wine that makes Chateau de Monbazillac so famous. There are 3500 hectares of vines which predominately produce the widely known sweet dessert white wines. The shop on site allows visitors to taste the various varieties of this extraordinary wine and of course make wine purchases which can be delivered across the world.

https://www.chateau-monbazillac.com

Chateau des Vigiers:

As already mentioned Chateau des Vigiers has three beautifully manicured golf courses, but the chateau itself has an interesting history. Jean Vigiers purchased the land from the Duchess de La Rochefoucauld in 1597. The chateau has been described as a "Petit Versailles" due to its classic architectural style of that time. The most striking element of the property is the dovecote commissioned in the 17th century by Jean Vigiers' daughter, Marguerite. The Chateau belonged to the Vigiers family until the French Revolution. The property then changed hands several times before a consortium of Swedes purchased the property to restore the chateau and gradually develop a high class hotel and restaurant which was completed in 1993. There is also the Church of Sainte-Croix located south of the chateau which dates from the 12th century and has interesting catacombs. The real estate developments at the Chateau have resulted in Residences du Lac, Allee des Vigiers and the Maria Galland Beauty Institute with a hydrotherapy pool. In 2014 Chef Didier Casaguana received his first Michelin star and the food both in the Hotel and the Golf Clubhouse is excellent.

https://www.vigiers.com.fr

Abbaye de Saint-Ferme:

The Abbaye is situated on the D16 between Pellegrue and Monsegur. Saint-Ferme itself is a commune in the Gironde region of Nouvelle-Aquitaine. The Catholic Benedictine Abbaye building is imposing, constructed in the 12th and 13th centuries. The church features a 12th century nave and very well preserved Romanesque capitals depicting Daniel and the Lions' den and the Presentation at the Temple. At the time of its use, the Abbaye had seven priories, eight mills and five huge cellars as well as significant land over six of the neighbouring parishes. During the Hundred Years War, the buildings were fortified and the moat was dug closer to the main Abbaye building. At the end of the 18th century, shortly before the French Revolution, the monks finally left the Abbaye which then became the property of the town inhabitants. The Abbaye still houses the town hall as well as a museum on monastic life. The interior of the Abbaye is intact and makes a great visit.

Although there are still many Abbeys active in France, particularly in the Normandy and Burgundy regions, there are virtually none in the Gironde region of SW France. There are many ruins to visit but it is sad to hear that the numbers of both Benedictine and Cistercian monks are reducing, mainly due to the monks dying and not being replaced by new brethren.

Plum Village in the tradition of Zen Master Thich Nhat Hanh:

Plum Village is located in the lower hamlet of Loubes-Bernac, a small hamlet near Ste-Foy-la-Grande. It is home to an international community whose practice is to dwell happily in the present moment whilst living out daily activities. Thich Nhat Hanh is a global spiritual leader, poet and peace activist, known for his pioneering teachings on Buddhism, global ethics and peace. Throughout the year Plum Village is open for retreats, allowing visitors to rest and heal themselves through mindful living. Visitors can include anyone who is in need of this calming and meditative environment and often includes nuns and monks as well as lay people. There is a five year monastic training programme available and there is detailed information on this programme on the website. On the day that I visited there was not a soul to be seen; it was raining and reception and other buildings were closed. As there was nobody around to speak to I didn't feel able to gain any real appreciation of what the centre was aiming to achieve, which was a great pity.

https://plumvillage.org

CHAPTER 6:
Discovering Chateau Feely, Chateau Carbonneau and other local vineyards.

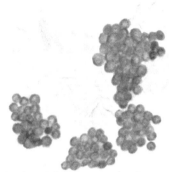

Du grain de raisin au verre de vin ...

Before we explore the various local vineyards, it is worth noting the differences between the two major wine growing regions of Bordeaux and Burgundy. Firstly looking at the amount of wine produced, Burgundy produces 185 million bottles per annum, the Bordeaux region produces 630 million bottles per annum, with the percentage of vineyards accounting for 3.6% of the land in Burgundy compared to 17% of the land in the Bordeaux region .However interestingly from the *terroir* of the Bordeaux region only two or three wines are produced, whereas in Burgundy each different climate produces a very specific wine. The red wines of Bordeaux are usually Merlot, Cabernet Sauvignon, Cabernet Franc or Petit Verdo; the white wines being Semillon, Sauvignon and Muscadelle. As I am starting this chapter with a visit to Chateau Feely, I should also add that the

Bordeaux region has four times as much area of land producing organically labelled wine

Chateau Feely in Saussignac

This is an interesting story of a family from Ireland who came to France 11 years ago, with the intention of buying a vineyard and turning it into an organic and biodynamic family wine business. Caro and Sean, her husband and their two daughters, Sophia and Ellie have worked tirelessly throughout the last decade to turn their land purchase into the very successful enterprise that it has become. When Sean and Caro moved to France, Ellie was a baby of a few months and Sophia was just starting school; both girls are now fluent in French and are totally immersed in their French way of life. Over the past 10 years Caro has written three books tracking the highs and lows of developing their business; the books are inspiring to read as they take the reader in a very honest and humorous way through their whole journey. Caro's repertoire as an author has further developed as she has become extraordinarily experienced in creating organic wines and has now published books on the detailed process of wines and their development. Life has been tough physically, mentally and financially, but they are an amazingly resilient family and against many odds they have come through the other side, not only surviving but creating some wonderful wines and an impressive business. I visited Chateau Feely in August and although I wasn't able to taste the wine, I still had the tour with the other visitors and was able to hear the background of their wine growing experiences from Caro, as she led us around parts of their estate. The tour gave me the added opportunity to view the building developments that have now been achieved at Chateau Feely.

Caro and Sean have put in a swimming pool and have developed ecological luxury self-catering *gites,* which are available to rent throughout the year. This combined with the opportunity for guided wine tours, tastings, wine and food pairing lunches and multi day walking tours offers a comprehensive holiday or day visit to this pretty village of Saussignac and the Chateau Feely estate.

https://www.chateaufeely.com
caro@chateaufeely.com

Chateau Carbonneau, near to Gensac (Ste-Foy-la-Grande)

This delightful chateau and its vineyards are owned by Wilfrid and Jacquie Franc de Ferriere, who with their four children have developed their business since 1995 into what is now a thriving success. The chateau was built in 1880 and is set in tranquil and glorious grounds covering two hectares of parkland with a large south facing swimming pool. The Chateau has five luxurious guest rooms and serves breakfast on the large terrace as well as in the dining room, with lunch and dinner served to both resident and non-resident guests. The vineyards cover a further 30 hectares shared with the Aquitaine Blond cattle who provide manure based fertiliser for the land. From Easter onwards, the proprietors open The Glass House, which serves delicious afternoon teas or indeed perhaps an early evening light supper, the country platters are enticing, delicious and available until 9pm. There are six main wines to taste, in the form of white, red and pink which are produced from grapes that are grown from a unique soil type which gives the *appellation* of Bordeaux its originality and elegance. A rather lovely touch is that the white and rose wines are named after Wilfred and Jacqui's two daughters, Margot (white) and Lulu (rose).

https://www.chateau-carbonneau.com
carbonneau@orange.fr (bed and breakfast bookings)
carbonneau.wine@orange.fr (wines and tastings)

Chateau La Tourbeille, Juillac, (Pessac)

Chateau La Tourbeille is a stunning18th century chateau located in the heart of the Bordeaux wine region, owned and run by a delightful English couple with their young family. With its luxurious facilities and perfect setting overlooking the Dordogne river, it is an ideal venue to hold a wedding, a yoga retreat, charity events, special parties or simply to rent the the entire 8 bedroomed Chateau for a large family holiday. The Chateau sleeps 16 people, has 10 bathrooms and is available throughout the year. Zaylie is a charming hostess and responds speedily to queries about bookings.

A recent development is that the owners of the Le Gensake restaurant in Gensac, have moved their premises to Pessac, and have established a restaurant base at Chateau La Tourbeille. They are open for lunch and dinner everyday, apart from Monday and Tuesdays. I have to add that to sit under an umbrella on the sunny terrace situated above the Dordogne river simply adds to the enjoyment of the delicious food.

https//:chateautourbeille.com
info@chateautourbeille.com

Under separate ownership is the nearby 100 acre La Tourbeille Vineyard which is owned by a French - American family, John Sandifer and his wife Mary Bruton Sandifer who by modernising the winery have developed superb award winning wines since 2012. Although it should be noted that the vineyard has been an esteemed wine making property since the early 1770's. The Sandifer children have now joined the family venture and between them they have worked together to produce some excellent wines. Especially renowned are La Tourbeille cuvée " Le Sceptre" and the "L'Esprit de Jeanne" selected as one of the top ten rosé wines of the Bordeaux region. The family also have holiday accommodation on their property and arrange wine tastings and other events.

https//:www.latourbeille.com

sandifer@latourbeille.com

Chateau Verriere Bellevue in Landerrouat

The owners of this vineyard are Dolores and Alain Bessette, a delightful couple who are very welcoming to visitors. With all vineyards that offer *dégustations* it is safer to ring and make an appointment for your time of arrival as many of the proprietors are out working on the vineyards during the day. The Bessette family have been making wines for four generations and have developed excellent white, rose and a selection of Bordeaux red wines. There is a small but attractive gift shop and a visit to this vineyard is good fun, perhaps en route to a visit to Duras.

https://www.chateaulaverriere.com

Chateau Grand Montet in St-Andre-et-Appelles

This vineyard was situated in our village and therefore we became quite friendly with Didier Roussel, who owns this *vignoble* with his wife Marie-France. Another charming French family who invite you to taste their range of wines with infectious enthusiasm. The vineyard produces white and red wines and a delicious Bordeaux Clairet. Clairet is a wine that is dark pink in colour and can be described as a full bodied rose. It is considered a specialty of the Bordeaux region and is thought to have originated in Quinsac in Premieres Cotes de Bordeaux. This delightful wine, when chilled, is perfect on a summer day, either drunk on its own, as an *apéritif* or to accompany a meal.

https://www.grandmontet.com

chateaugrandmontet@orange.fr

Chateau Jaron in Landerrouat

This vineyard was another favourite to visit and is owned by Caroline and Philippe Liberatore. Philippe began developing the family business in 1994, which, after he married Caroline Comin in 1998, became the Vignobles Comin-Liberatoire. The young couple have brought modern techniques to the wine making process and an interesting tour led by Caroline tells of their progress. Apart from ageing the wine partially in stainless steel vats, it is also aged in clay amphorae (jugs) for 12 months, giving the red wine a distinctive flavour of crushed strawberry /raspberry. We also tasted a stunning sweet wine which surprisingly was recommended to drink with Roquefort cheese.

https://www.chateau-jaron.fr

philippe.liberatore@orange.fr

This is just a sample of the vineyards local to to St André et Appelles, although there are indeed thousands of vineyards in the Bordeaux region, with each village surrounded by them. The majority are open for tastings and purchases, with appointments booked by telephone.

The next four chapters describe in more detail the main city of Bordeaux and the towns of Bergerac, St Emilion and Ste-Foy-la-Grande. It would be quite remiss of me to produce lengthy detailed information on any of these places, as the national and international guide books comprehensively describe these towns in great detail. The Rough Guide and Lonely Planet guide books also include how to travel to and from these different towns by car, rail and air, and helpfully suggest accommodation and eating options. Regardless of this, I wanted to share my impressions and alert readers to elements of the towns that we particularly enjoyed when visiting in both the summer and winter months.

CHAPTER 7:
Bordeaux

Bordeaux is the sixth largest metropolitan area in France, after Paris, Marseille, Lyon, Toulouse and Lille. It is the capital of the Nouvelle Aquitaine region and a city well worth visiting. Being at the centre of a major wine growing area, it exercises significant influence in the world of wine. However the historic part of the city is on the UNESCO World Heritage List and visitors would be advised to allow some hours exploring the city in some depth. Bordeaux is classified as a city of Art and History, and boasts 362 historical monuments.

The challenge with Bordeaux, like other cities, is the traffic when attempting to get in and out of the city. There is an effective ring road where the traffic usually continues to move but the driver has to concentrate as the cars, motorhomes and lorries often drive head to tail. Certainly allow more time than is needed if your journey involves travelling to the Airport.

Bordeaux Airport

The airport is easy to find, well signposted and about 15 mins from the city centre. However despite the size of the city it is a relatively small airport and facilities are somewhat limited. Saying that, car parking is close to the main terminal building, so access is easy and parking is not expensive.

In the summer, it is almost too hot to explore museums and galleries, although of course everywhere is beautifully air conditioned and very comfortable. However, although Bordeaux has some wonderful treasures to discover and explore, we found that we wanted to simply stroll around the city enjoying the ambience and local pleasures, stopping fairly regularly for a coffee, or a beer, or a glass of wine.

St Catherine's Street

This is the longest shopping street in France and is a real mixture of typical city stores and delightful smaller boutique shops with more unusual items to purchase. I found a lovely shop which sold very attractive swimsuits, in a range of sizes, styles and colours. Swimsuits are items not sold on local market stalls in the villages and this was one of my reasons for visiting Bordeaux.

The English Bookshop (Bradley's)

The English Bookshop situated on Rue de la Merci is small and intimate; it is a short diversion off St Catherine's Street to pop in and browse along the bookshelves. Visitors are welcome to sit and have a coffee as they explore the many selections of books on offer. It was when I was visiting this bookshop that I was surprised to discover that there are so few guide books on the more rural areas of this beautiful area of France, which abounds with culture and history. Back on St Catherine's Street interspersed between the shops are tiny cafes with shaded tables on the pavement, offering a range of delicious morsels. My sister and I had sardines, which came as an opened tin of sardines, a lemon cut in two halves and delicious fresh bread for mopping up the sardine oil. Just perfect for a light lunch in the shaded warmth of a side street, my sister thoroughly enjoying a chilled Sauvignon Blanc, whilst I had the obligatory carafe of sparkling water!

Sainte-Andre Cathedral

The area around the Sainte-Andre Cathedral is a large and attractive open space, overlooking the town hall with the French flag blowing proudly in the breeze, where the trams runs close by, and how gorgeous, there appeared around the corner a yellow CV just like the one I owned when I was a student physiotherapist! There are lots of outdoor cafes and bars and a large market bookstall set up under shady umbrellas selling mainly second hand books and black and white sketches of bygone years in France. The Cathedral is notable because of its free standing bell tower, although it was far too hot to even contemplate climbing all those stairs to get to the top; people emerging from the tower ecstatically described the spectacular views and, although somewhat breathless from the climb and the heat, highly recommended making the effort…

Saint-Andre

The Cathedral of the Archbishops of Bordeaux, was built between the 12th and14th centuries. Eleanor of Aquitaine and Louis VII were married here in 1137, as were Anne of Austria and Louis XIII. Sadly the Cathedral suffered from a devastating fire in the 19th century, but all of the furniture and fittings were replaced mainly, rumour has it, by removing possessions from other churches. Barthelemy Marcade, a Bordelais who went to Paris to become a priest, was also an art lover who collected holy antiques from the 14th to 17th centuries.In 1947, before his death he donated his entire collection to the nation and this has latterly been placed on public view in the Cathedral.

During the summer, there is a season of sacred music festivals held at the Cathedral. As with all events across the City information can be obtained from the well-stocked Tourist Office.

Apart from The Cathedral other similar religious buildings to visit include:

- **- Basilica Saint Seurin**
- **- Basilica Saint Michel**

The Quayside

The Quayside has been developed over the past three years; indeed there is lots of construction work still happening, but that was another great area to amble through. One of the most amazing sights on the Quayside is the **Cité du Vin,** the largest wine museum in the world. The very hot day when we were in Bordeaux and the length of the queue to get in, rather reluctantly made us decide that this would be a tour to do on my return in January. (see chapter 15)

All in all, Bordeaux is a charming city and there are masses of interesting things to do, book a boat trip, visit the famous "water mirror", relax in one of the many parks, climb the 229 steps up the Pey-Berland tower (!) visit the Darwin Ecosysteme, the alternative place on the right bank of the river, the Opera House or simply enjoy the unique atmosphere of old Bordeaux.

One thing to note is that from Bordeaux it is a straightforward drive to Archachon and the enormous sand dunes on the west coast, plus the divine and numerous fresh fish restaurants that abound the Atlantic coastline.

It was actually in Bordeaux sitting in the shade outside a cafe, that a butterfly landed on my unused wine glass. There was a small jug of lavender on the table and this beautiful white butterfly fluttered around our table for several minutes before settling on the lavender flowers. I quietly watched this exquisite creature trying not to frighten it off, but it was in no hurry to move whatsoever. It seemed such a special moment, just this white butterfly and me ….and in that moment I realised that this had to be the title of my book.

I was sufficiently enthralled with the encounter that when I arrived back home early that evening , I googled " the butterfly" and learned some interesting facts for budding lepidopterists:-

- Butterfly wings are transparent as they are made up by layers of a protein called chitin.
- Butterflies taste with their feet, a female drums the leaves with her feet until plant juices are released. When she identifies the right match of plant chemicals on the leaf she lays her eggs.

- Butterflies live on all liquid diet, usually nectar.
- A butterfly must assemble its own proboscis (mouthparts) quickly, otherwise it will starve.
- Butterflies drink from mud puddles, as they cannot live on sugar alone, also needing minerals and salts both nutrients which are found in mud puddles.
- Butterflies cannot fly if they are cold below, 55F, nor when they first emerge from the chrysalis.
- Butterflies often live for just a few weeks, during that time it focuses on eating and mating.
- Butterflies are shortsighted, but can see colours some that are invisible to the human eye.

I should clarify that Bordeaux is not a city known for its butterflies! Although it is common to see paper confetti for weddings in the shape of butterflies which are referred to as "Bordeaux Butterflies".

The Museum of Science and Nature situated at 5, Place Bardineau houses examples of butterflies and a vast range of other insects. Workshops are held, especially for senior visitors where time is taken to learn more about them and observe these creatures at close quarters.

CHAPTER 8:
Bergerac

Bergerac is known for its old town's half-timbered buildings and the castles that dot the local countryside. Bergerac is designated as a town of art and history. The town has a growing tourist industry with wine tours, chateau visits, the town museum, the statue museum and the tobacco museum. Bergerac is also situated on the Dordogne River and offers opportunities for canoeing and kayaking, cycling and walking.

Gabare de la Dordogne

Another way to explore the magnificent scenery of the Dordogne River is aboard a *gabare*, a traditional flat bottomed wooden cargo barge used for transporting goods downstream to Bordeaux. By 1850, river transport accounted for 60% of the merchandise trade between Bergerac and Bordeaux. Wine accounted for the largest share of the traffic. Nowadays a guided boat trip starting from Bergerac is a wonderful way to enjoy the spectacular views of the villages and chateaux along the river, and to discover the fauna and flora of the River Dordogne that has been classified as a World Biosphere Reserve by UNESCO.

Bergerac also has a wide selection of shops, cafes and restaurants and it is easy to spend a day in this lovely old town. Where we staying in St-Andre-et-Appelles was ideally suited for **Bergerac Airport (Bergerac Dordogne Perigord).** During our two months' stay, several friends and family came over to visit us. Bordeaux airport was 90 mins away, whilst Bergerac airport was 30 mins drive, so we encouraged visitors whenever possible to book their flights to Bergerac Airport. We must have gone to and fro the airport at least a dozen times, but it was perfectly situated on the Ste-Foy-la-Grande side of Bergerac and an attractive drive. The airport is very small but has a tiny restaurant with delicious pastries and coffee, so sitting in the sunshine watching for the dot of the aeroplane to appear in the cloudless blue sky was quite delightful, reminding us again and again how lucky we were to be discovering this unspoilt area of SW France. Visitors would arrive already looking relaxed and quite delighted to land, pass through passport control and collect their luggage in 10 - 15 minutes. Walking to the car in the warm sunshine and being offered a stop for a quick beer or coffee on the way back to the house seemed to suit most people. What a perfect start to a holiday!

I should add that one friend who was due to join us for a week around my birthday celebrations was sadly stuck on the M5 in Devon for five hours due to a fatality which closed the motorway. Josie consequently missed her flight!

CHAPTER 9:
Sainte-Foy-la-Grande

Ste-Foy-la-Grande is a commune in the Gironde department of Nouvelle-Aquitaine. It is in the arrondissement of Libourne, some 20 kilometres along the road towards Bordeaux. It is a pretty town situated on the banks of the Dordogne with a population of between 2,000 and 3,000. Ste-Foy-la-Grande is another attractive walled *bastide* town which still retains many of its original medieval buildings. It rather unusually has the Dordogne River actually splitting the town so it is on both banks of the river. Across the bridge to Port Ste Foy there is also a small river beach, *Plage de Bardoulets,* where people can at least paddle and cool off on a hot day.

Ste-Foy-la-Grande has one of the **best markets** in the region, and on a Saturday morning the town is teeming with locals and tourists coming many miles to shop. The stalls include the usual range of fresh vegetables, fruit and flowers, but also a wide selection of highly coloured clothes stalls, with dresses, shirts and skirts to suit every size and taste. Pottery and other artisan craft stalls are in abundance as are willow baskets, linen tablecloths and bed linen. Cafes and bars abound in the covered archways, where people, having completed their shopping, enjoy a coffee, pastry or glass of wine.

Much of the building in the town dates back to the 15th century with half-timbered houses and sculptured beams on the outside. The town has prospered as the centuries passed, mainly due the port and the local wine trade. Certainly Ste Foy is a good stopping place to explore the local Bordeaux wine region.

The nearby **Chateau de Montaigne** is an impressive building with magnificent grounds and it is worth a trip across the river to visit this property, which was once the home of the French Renaissance writer Michel de Montaigne.

Ste Foy la Grande is a good place to visit on a rainy day, as there are several interesting churches to visit and lots of cafe's and restaurants to enjoy afterwards.

Eglise Notre Dame is the main Catholic Church of this attractive town, situated on Rue des Frères-Reclus. It was built in the 13th century and dedicated to the Virgin Mary. The first church was destroyed by the Huguenots in 1561, but rebuilt between 1622 and 1686. The only areas of the original building that remain are the base of the bell tower, the oratory, the chapel of the baptismal font and the tribune, all of which are in Romanesque style.

The Protestant Temple is located in Rue Louis Pasteur and is attached to the United Protestant Church of France. This church was founded in Set Foy la Grande in 1558 and a provincial synod took place there in 1561. However the temple was destroyed in 1683 when the Protestant troops were defeated by the royal armies under Louis XIII. A new church was built on the same site in 1686. It is worth viewing the organ which is an Alsatian instrument installed in1842 and renovated by the Gers organ builder Patrice Bellet in 1995.

Cave Larégnère is a good place to explore for all of the varied wines available, the large selection of beers and spirits and the different glassware and carafes to purchase. There is a stall of local food products, with a special emphasis on cheese and chocolates; certainly an excellent shop to while away an hour or so!

CHAPTER 10:
St Emilion

St Emilion is a gem of a town in the Gironde region. It is rich in history and historical events as well as being famous for its Grand Cru wines, along with its neighbouring village, Pomerol. The town of St Emilion was born in 767, when the disciples of Emilianus buried his body in the Oratory and decided to carry on his saintly work in the local vicinity. The story of Emilianus is a local legend and worthy of sharing with you.

Emilianus

Emilianus was born in Brittany in the 8th century. He left his humble family to work for the Count of Vannes, who found Emilianus to be a man of great piety and humility. Later Emilianus went on a pilgrimage to Santiago de Compostela. The journey was long and arduous and Emilianus made a stop at the Saujon monastery at Saintes, and after a while he made great friends with the Prior of the Abbey. The other monks subsequently became jealous of his extreme piety and friendship with the Prior. So another move resulted and Emilianus continued on his journey following the Dordogne River. On the heights above Peyrefitte, he found a cliff face which he converted into a living cave combined with an oratory in the corner. Here Emilianus found the perfect place to meditate and retired from the world filling his days with fasting and prayer, and as a result he felt great peace of mind and close to God. However as people began to know of his existence, they visited him in his cave where he performed miracles of healing. Once a blind woman had a dream that Emilianus had traced a cross on her head and she regained her sight. This had happened as she dreamt about visiting Emilianus in his cave where he was impressed by her faith, and the woman experienced the miracle of seeing once more. Emilianus however grew tired of all of his visitors and begged God "to take him out of this valley of tears...". A few days later after a short illness he died as he had wished and his legacy was born in this famous town of St Emilion.

There is so much history to St Emilion that a guide book focused on this town is absolutely essential and a whole range of books and maps can be purchased from the busy *office de tourism* in the main square. Suffice to say that it is difficult to ever tire of a visit to this charming place.

The Collegiate Church of St Emilion

This is one of the largest and most beautiful churches in the Gironde region. The building was begun in the 12th century and extended further in the 14th century. When you stand at the cord preventing access to the choir, visitors see Emilianus above them holding a book and appearing to smile down at them… there are three other depictions of Emilianus in the Church. One aspect not to be missed when visiting the church is a walk along the cloister corridor. This was where the monks promenaded in the winter and there are still benches dotted along its length for the monks to rest. In times past the cloister was adorned with murals and, although most of the paintings have now disappeared, the remains are still worth viewing.

The Bell Tower of St Emilion is the highest in the Gironde after the Saint-Michel bell tower in Bordeaux. The monolithic church sits below it, and the bell tower stands 53 metres from the floor of the church. It is permissible to climb the tower and thankfully at the top there is a balustrade to keep viewers safe. One of the functions of the bell tower was to be a landmark for pilgrims travelling to Santiago de Compostela.

The Monolithic Church

This is dug out of the cliff and is another sight to visit in this wonderful town. Underground churches are rare in France and the church of St Emilion is the largest in Europe. The entrance to the church is from the market place square and this space was originally the church graveyard. There is a legend that if an autumn leaf falls and sits on the shoulder of a visitor drinking coffee on the terrace, it is the spirit of one of the elders joining the guests at the table.

St Emilion is built on a rocky amphitheatre and with the houses of golden stone and tiled roofs seemingly changing colour during the day as the sun changes its position, it is just a perfect place to wander round. The cobbled streets add to overall charm of the town, but do wear comfortable and flat shoes, as the cobbles can be uneven and the town is hilly in parts. Certainly beware in the rain!

Brunet Gate

Brunet Gate is only one of the original gates into the town; it is worth a visit for the views over the town and surrounding countryside, and can be easily walked to within 5-10 minutes of leaving the tourist office. Apart from the views, once you have passed through the gate, there are vineyards where you can walk the dog and, better still, cars parked along the grass verges can be left there for free.

Place de Marché

Place de Marché, where the market place is situated is a bustling square, even when there is no market. This is a convenient place to meet up for a coffee, a glass of wine or beer but tables get taken very quickly in the summer; there are lots of other cafes in the little side streets and it is worth wandering off the beaten track a little. Also prices are slightly reduced away from the key tourist areas of the town centre.

The Cordeliers' Cloister

This was founded as a convent by Franciscan brothers in the 13th century. A second convent was then established in the 14th century. The site was sold as a national property in 1791 due to the its state of disrepair, but has now been developed into a tranquil haven of peace where it is possible to tour the buildings, visit the shop, eat in the garden or simply sample a chilled glass of the superb " Cremant de Bordeaux". The building is closed in the winter months so make this a summer visit.

Steep street steps.

These are referred to as " Tertres" and are situated in the town allowing people to walk safely between the upper and lower levels. The cobbles are attractive and there are tiny shops situated either side of the street as you make your descent . However beware on a rainy day as the cobblestones become very slippery. Ascending is often the safer option !

This is only a sample of what St Emilion has to offer and it is a town to explore at leisure. One cannot walk around St Emilion without noticing that every other shop sells wine, glasses and splendidly designed decanters! Enter these shops at your peril unless you are expecting to leave with some very expensive purchases. It is quite permissible to taste the wines on offer but there is now a charge as many of the tourists will not actually be looking to buy the wines, which often start at 40-50 euros a bottle, and rise to thousands of euros for the grand cru varieties. During the summer the charge was around five euros to "taste" two different wines which will be selected by the owner. For wine tasting, *dégustation,* it is far better to go to vineyards well away from St Emilion, unless you are a true connoisseur of fine wines and a serious purchaser.

A few suggestions of places to have a coffee or a light bite include:

- **Chai Pascal,** in the heart of the village; this is a restaurant and a wine bar, where you can get a delicious and very reasonable glass of wine.

- **Le Bonheur** is a small snack bar, almost opposite Chai Pascal. There are two or three tables outside, with four or five tables inside. Food can be eaten on the premises or can be taken away. The owners are very friendly and the coffee is delicious.

- **Restaurant le Medieval**, at the foot of the village, in the Place de la Porte Bouqueyre, was recommended by the tourist office but the day we visited the restaurant was closed.

- **La Terrasse Rouge** at Chateau la Dominque is good place for lunch.

St Emilion is a very popular place to visit and it is better to go earlier in the day in the summer months, before it gets too packed and also too hot. However I was very surprised when I returned to write my winter chapter in January, how quiet it actually was. Many hotels, restaurants and shops are closed for the month of January although the main tourist attractions are all open and a delight to visit as they are so uncrowded.

CHAPTER 11:
Arts and Crafts

Orchestre de Chambre de la Gironde: Music

These annual musical festivals are hugely popular and offer the public the opportunity to enjoy familiar works of Mozart, Debussy and Haydn but also those of less famous composers such as Nielson, Volkmann, Finzi, Sarasate and Glass. This highly accomplished orchestra led by Scott Sandmeier performs in the beautiful churches of the Gironde villages, with additional concerts held in local parklands, combined with an evening musical stroll through the grounds. These concerts are combined with *apéritifs* and opportunities for the audience to mingle and chat to members of the Orchestra. Scott Sandmeier came to France from the US, to follow the masterclasses of Leonard Bernstein and Jean-Sebastion Bereau. He is assistant conductor at the National Orchestra of Lyon and performs with many French orchestras and has been artistic director of the Gironde Chamber Orchestrated the Gensac Festival since 1991. www.orchestredechambredelagironde.fr

Claire Scofield: Painting

Claire is a well-known artist in the Gironde. In the spring of 2017 Claire created an art studio in Pellegrue to devote herself completely to her painting. I came across Claire's work when I was visiting the area in 2018. Claire was running an exhibition of her paintings in Monsegur after she had recently completed a series of watercolours of various scenes in the Jardin de Sardy. I was particularly struck with one view across the lake, which captured the evening light on a set of cobbled steps leading to a house window which was surrounded by wisteria. Since making that purchase I have followed Claire's work with great interest and have been impressed with her versatility.

I have included a short biography for your interest, especially if you are an art lover.

Claire showed a keenness for art since she was a small girl when she loved the smell of the oil paints in her uncle's workshop and studio in Paris, where he was a restorer of original art works. Her love of drawing and art materials grew and Claire subsequently studied art at the University of Bordeaux and went on to teach art in secondary schools. As a talented artist Claire frequently takes part in art exhibitions with other local artists in the Bordeaux region. Claire lives in the heart of Pellegrue with her husband Barry, a guitar playing British singer and songwriter. Unusually in the basement of their house, Barry has set up a recording studio, nicknamed The Twilight Zone, in which he composes and creates his songs. Claire, a talented singer too, performs with Barry as a harmonising musical duo who perform in local cafes and bars during the summer months.
atelier.scofield@gmail.com

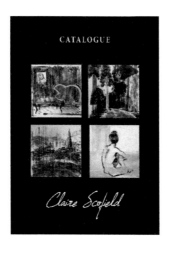

Emmanuel Michel: Sculpture

This gifted man was born in 1970 and has developed as a painter, and creator of oriental and African sculptures which include humans and animals in living poses. For 30 years he has dedicated himself to drawing, engraving, painting and sculpting inspired by the years of travelling on five continents. Throughout the years he has held many exhibitions both in France and around the world. Emmanuel has also written 10 books on his work. In 2015 he created the Jarkhot Publishing House. I visited Emmanuel's exhibition at Vigiers in 2019, and it was fascinating to view his creativity and the intricate detail of his models.

www. emmanuelmichel.com

emmanuel.michel0055@orange.fr

Sylvain Drouot: Pottery and ceramics

Sylvain is a skilled potter who has introduced modern techniques into his repertoire .His versatility is illustrated by his range of plates, serving bowls , unusually shaped egg cups , jugs etc, which are attractive to purchase for personal use or as holiday gifts for friends and family. Sylvain has a stall at the weekly markets of Eymet, Riberac, Ste-Foy-la-Grande and Issigeac.
sdpoterie@orange.fr

Theatres and Cinemas

There are cinemas in almost every village, small and intimate but with an interesting selection of films, some may have English subtitles, although the film itself will be in French. Theatres can be found in the larger towns and cities. The type of productions will be varied and tourist offices will have all of this local information. Often in the summer months, some plays and productions will be adapted to be outdoors, so bring a blanket and a cushion! Some chateau gardens hosting an event will often offer food or allow people to bring a picnic.

Jazz Festivals and other musical events

A range of musical events are offered through the summer in most villages and towns. Often a musical evening or local dance is attached to evening markets, where entire families come to buy food and drink and join in with all the townsfolk. These evenings are fun and have a real *joie de fête* atmosphere and are great opportunity to join in with the local entertainment.

Jazz evenings and festivals are very common in this area of SW France with skilled musicians coming from all over France for these special events which often run for a week at a time.

CHAPTER 12:
Eating out in the summer

"She visits my town once a year, she fills my mouth with kisses and nectar, I spend all my money on her … who man, your girl?"

"No, a mango!"

Amir Khusro

French cuisine and I are a perfect match. I love it. I love the regional specialties, the fish soups, the chowders and the fish stews; the meat and poultry variations and the wonderful sauces that accompany each dish. I am a great cheese fan, so in the winter *fondues, raclettes* and *tartiflettes* suit me perfectly and as I cannot resist the smell of gruyere and emmental cheese cooking - walking past a restaurant specialising in hot cheese dishes would always entice me in. When I was younger the smell of Gauloise cigarettes had a similar effect! I am equally enthralled by the range of wonderful succulent looking vegetables and fruit, there is so much one can do to make a relatively simple meal look and taste superb.

Every village has a restaurant / cafe that would be very acceptable to eat at. This of course is France and wherever we stopped for a light bite, lunch or dinner the food was delightful, fresh and tasty. Meal times are to be enjoyed in France, are always leisurely and to be savoured. The selection of local wines was immense and whether you were drinking red, white or rose there was always a new wine to savour. Therefore this following selection of restaurants are but a few in the area that we visited and particularly enjoyed.

Palma Nova in Pessac

A small but very friendly restaurant on the banks of the Dordogne at Pessac. It is run by a very helpful and jolly band of young people who focus their dishes on cheese ingredients and fish. The menu is not extensive but the food is delicious, well presented and served with a smile. It has a lovely setting and one can sit and enjoy the canoeists returning from their day on the river as the sun sets. It is open at lunchtime and in the evening and provides a good value *plat du jour*.

Le Gensake: Gensac

A typically French village restaurant with tables on the pavement under colourful umbrellas. It has a good range of local food and diners can enjoy the comings and goings in the village whilst eating. Gensac is a small but pretty village and worth a diversion to visit. It also has a lovely old church which hosts some of the Gensac music festival concerts.

Le café de Paris: Gensac

This cafe has the appearance of a bar / cafe where you might stop and have a casual drink, but the *Monsieur* cooks the most delicious omelettes! The menu also contains other straightforward fare but the meals are well cooked, tasty and very good value for money.

Le Mekong Chinese restaurant: Pineuilh (Ste-Foy-la-Grande)

A great choice for a group of friends in the evening, who are hungry and simply want to enjoy some very good Chinese food. Customers pay a set price and basically help themselves to as much as they can eat. There is a very varied selection of meat, fish and vegetarian options. The staff are very welcoming and when guests ask for their Wok dish, it is cooked for them at the open plan 'wok cooking area' in front of the guests. Very good value and a great family outing.

Le Sympa: St Vivien de Monsegur

This restaurant is a real treasure of a place; situated in a small but attractive hamlet some four to five miles from Monsegur. From the outside it looks like a typical cafe where you might stop for a drink in the evening sunshine, sipping drinks at the table on the pavement outside the front door. But then you go inside, through the bar and into a dining room with five tables, probably able to accommodate 15 - 20 people in total. The *Monsieur* is the chef in the family kitchen, whilst *Madame* takes our orders and brings us an *apéritif.* There are local food specialties to choose from as starters and main courses. The gambas prawns are superb, but all the dishes were beautifully cooked. A carafe of wine of a colour of your choice is given to the table free-gratis. After the starter and main course the cheese board arrives which is feast of delicious looking cheese and *Madame* generously offers you whichever cheeses you would like to sample. After this feast we really felt we would have to pass on the dessert course, until we spied what the customers on the adjoining table were eating …scrumptious light and fluffy *tartes* and *mousses* which looked irresistible! Certainly no room for coffee at the end, only the bill. It was all so reasonable for the quality of food we had happily consumed.

As a bonus in the summer months on a Friday night the restaurant hosts a *Soiree Tapas,* I am sure it would be a really tasty, very generous and enjoyable experience.

La Maison Vari: Monbazillac

We discovered this restaurant one lunchtime after visiting the chateau in the morning. This is a wine bar, restaurant and shop. The interior is attractively designed and has the appearance of being in a friend's kitchen cum dining room. The menu is not extensive although there were some local specialties, true to form the food was well presented and delicious. I was assured by members of my family that the wines were very good and I bought a few gifts, like unusual wine coolers, from the in house shop. There is live music in the summer and the small restaurant can also be booked for private parties. Lunch was a most enjoyable experience.

Le Lion d'Or: Saussignac

We found this *auberge* with its pretty umbrellas and colourful tablecloths, quite by chance as we were en route to visit Chateau Feely, situated in the same village. The tables are arranged outside the restaurant on the small village square. The owner was charming and very welcoming and the food was as excellent as we had come to expect across this area of France. Salads are particularly delicious and always contain very fresh and interesting ingredients, and served with an omelette make just a perfect lunchtime meal. Then of course there are always the scrumptious French fries that accompany meat or fish. Starters usually appeal to us rather than a dessert, but the *mousse au chocolate* looked particularly tempting. We passed on this occasion only to complete our meal with a delightful French coffee and homemade *petits fours*.

La Terrasse: Duras

This was a restaurant we visited several times, both at lunchtime and in the evening. We were always welcomed by the owner with a smile and an invitation to choose our table. During the summer months the restaurant is very busy and it is important to make a reservation both for lunch and dinner. The specialties on the chalk board are always a great choice although the regular daily menu is excellent. My favourite was the lamb shank, the meat falling off the bone and served in a rich red wine *jus* . There is a large terrace in front of the restaurant which is very popular for lunchtime dining. The restaurant overlooks the Chateau of Duras which is an added bonus.

L'Ardoise: Pessac sur Dordogne

This is a more formal restaurant with prices that reflect its higher quality food. A place to go perhaps for a special lunch or dinner. The terrace has tubs of flowers and tables laid up attractively for diners, with the inside of the restaurant equally delightful. The menu looked sophisticated and delicious. Although we had been recommended to come and eat here, because I wasn't drinking alcohol or able to tolerate rich food, it did not seem a good choice on this visit.

L'Atelier de Candale

This restaurant and its sublime terrace with the most wonderful views over the vineyards of the Dordogne valley is slightly outside St Emilion, (five minutes in the car from the town centre) and is just a treat to visit especially at lunchtime. It is wise to book as this restaurant is very popular throughout the year. This is my favourite restaurant in both summer and winter. There are several complete menus depending on how hungry you are, how much you want to spend or an *a la carte* menu. Of course at lunchtime there is a very delicious *plat du jour* selection. The wines are exquisite and reasonable value considering that the restaurant is surrounded by Grand Cru vineyards. The sommelier will be very helpful in suggesting a good wine to accompany your meal at an affordable price.

Before sampling your favourite wines in any restaurant, it is interesting to observe the thickness and size of the wine glass. You will notice that restaurants usually offer smaller white wine glasses than red wine glasses, the purpose of this is to maintain the lower temperature of the white wine. The weight of the wine glass gives an impression of the elegance and finesse of the wine; a customer would not expect to drink from a heavy wine glass which might denote a rougher house wine. The thinner the edge of the glass the rim the better; this allows for less contact between the wine and your lips promoting greater appreciation of texture of the wine. Finally the narrower the glass, the more concentrated will be the aromas of the wine.

The last item to mention, but very important for a *chef,* is a visit to the local *Magasin de Couteaux* or *La Quincailleries* (hardware store). Knives are critical tools for the French cook. Each region uses their own particular brand and in the Gironde, Acquitaine and Dordogne areas you would expect to see *le montron, le caronnais* and *le violon* version of knives!

CHAPTER 13:
An eventful journey back to England

So, now it is time to return to England, the time has flown by and it has been a marvellous experience exploring this region of SW France and discovering new sights, talented people and the friendliness and welcome from the local population. Our visitors have been a delight to have to stay and despite the fact that I was the only member of my family not to be drinking a glass of champagne on my birthday, I will hopefully be able to make up for it when I return in January……for return I must to write my observations on being here in SW France during a potentially cold and wet winter month.

So on a lovely warm and sunny afternoon at the end of August, we packed both our cars with great precision and loaded to the hilt set off from our "home" in St André et Appelles and headed towards Bordeaux, where we would pick up the N10 and the autoroute northwards in the direction of the ferry port at Roscoff. One very useful idea when travelling on the French autoroutes is to purchase the Emovis Tag, which fits on the windscreen and allows you to pass through the *péages* on the autoroute without queueing to pay the toll. The CTV camera merely photographs the Emovis Tag on the windscreen and then invoices the car owners bank account at the end of the month. If you are driving in separate right handed English cars as we were, it saves the disruption of getting out of the vehicle either to pick up your ticket, or to pay the toll at the other end, especially with impatient drivers queuing behind you!

I had Harry in the car with me, Mike had a heavier load of wine and also his golf clubs which he had insisted on bringing to France, despite only playing twice in two months as it was far too hot. We had decided not to follow each other as it was over

100 miles to our overnight hotel, so I set off first with Mike 15-20 mins behind me. Both cars felt heavy from all of the luggage so we had agreed that neither of us would rush and meet up for dinner at our overnight Hotel in St Coutant le Grande.

I was an hour into my journey and nearing the N10, when Mike rang me on my hands free mobile to tell me that he had had a puncture. He would need roadside assistance to change the tyre so I should keep going and he might be a little late for dinner, but would join me as soon as he was able. Two hours later Mike rang again, the roadside assistance man had been very helpful but not only was the tyre punctured, the actual wheel was damaged too and the car was undrivable.

I was now nearing the turn off at Saintes, there was nothing I could do to improve this situation, my car was completely full, even the front passenger seat was piled up with luggage, so there was no point whatsoever in me retracing my steps to the outskirts of Bordeaux. Mike had no alternative but to watch his car being loaded on to a breakdown truck, taken to a garage, and the garage owner locking up the car saying that "tomorrow Monsieur we start a two week holiday, but we will take great care of your car, and repair it when the new wheel arrives." The European AA people then had to be called to take Mike from this garage to an overnight hotel nearby. Another two hours passed with Mike sitting on the pavement outside a closed garage, with his overnight bag, his golf shoes, his laptop and his golf clubs. It was now nine o'clock however the AA were very helpful taking Mike and his luggage to a reasonable hotel on the edge of the campus of Bordeaux airport - by now I guess he must have been very tempted to simply fly back to England, but the AA had promised to sort out a taxi the next morning to take Mike to a local car hire firm , so that he could at least complete his drive to Roscoff.

In the meantime I had arrived at the "Logis du Péré" hotel outside of the tiny hamlet of St Coutant le Grand. The road sign directions to the hotel were appalling and as it was situated far down a country lane, I wasted a considerable amount of time reversing backwards and forwards up and down single lane tracks. However once I arrived I was staggered that this stunning hotel existed in what seemed to be miles from civilisation. It is described in the *Michelin* as *"demeure historique"* built originally in the 14th century. What a treat this was going to be, Harry and I looked at each other happily and then remembered Mike sitting on the pavement in Bordeaux…. I explained to *Monsieur* that it would be only Harry and I staying the night and I would require a table for one on the terrace for dinner. I was shown to our ground floor very spacious suite and promised a table on the terrace for 8pm. The meal was perfect, delicious flavours, attractively presented and all in the midst of the gorgeous setting of this chateau and its grounds. I was slightly concerned at the thought of the bill arriving, but it was very reasonable, so too was the accommodation as we had clearly been upgraded from our original booking. Poor Mike, he would have loved this stay and felt it was a perfect end to our two months in France.

The next morning Harry had a good run in the open fields surrounding the hotel and then after his breakfast I loaded the car and we set off to continue our journey to Roscoff. I still had 555 kilometres to do, which I estimated would take almost 6 hours with stops for Harry. He was so good in the car but the weather was still hot and he needed sufficient water and breaks. An hour into the journey and I received my first call of many from Mike. The taxi had arrived to take him to the car hire firm at the airport, wonderful news until Mike asked why they were driving away from Bordeaux airport, *"Oh non Monsieur, nous allons a l'aeroport de Bergerac pour la voiture"*……so another 125 kilometres and nearly 2 hours driving retracing the journey we had both done yesterday back past St André et Appelles to Bergerac airport!

I am now safely progressing on my very smooth journey to Roscoff, wondering when I will ever see my husband again. The ferry was leaving Roscoff at 10pm, so on arrival I had time for a walk with Harry on the beach and to grab a bite to eat before joining the queue at the ferry port. I had received brief messages in the day that indicated Mike was at last driving to Roscoff, where he would leave the hire car and come onto the boat as a walking passenger. I really didn't hold out much hope that he would arrive and thank goodness he had his own passport and ferry ticket. As the time for boarding approached the cars all started up their engines as the queue began to inch forward for loading when lo and behold, this exhausted vision appeared at my car window. I am not sure what the other car passengers made of all of this but it didn't matter, Mike was thankfully there! We quickly squashed his belongings next to Harry, leaving Mike with his golf clubs to walk on as a foot passenger, from the entrance to the ships' loading ramp I wound down my window and shouted out " the cabin number is 7321!" On reflection I am certain that other passengers were certain that I had met a male stranger and was offering him a bed for the night! *Tant pis* the next morning as we docked at Plymouth at 6.30am, our wonderful neighbour was thankfully there to meet us off the boat and to give Mike a lift home.

It would be far too tedious to relate the events of the next few months but suffice to say that we arrived home on the 1st September and Mike had his car returned to our house on 26th November!

However the bookings are made for my return to SW France on the 2nd January 2020. I was a little unsure of a ferry crossing across the Channel at that time of the year, so I will be taking

Harry but this time I am driving to Folkestone; we are going through the Euro Tunnel and then driving through France, with one overnight stop en route.

So until January, *Joyeux Noel et à bientôt.*

CHAPTER 14:
Returning to France for the month of January

Wow! What a contrast to the summer months…

I arrived in thick mist and drizzle, driving the last 50 miles from Angoulême through deserted and twisting French country lanes, as Sat Nav had "told" me this was the quickest route! In 28 miles I drove through village after village, hamlet after hamlet and saw no-one at all. Houses and chateaux shuttered up, soggy wet fields, depressing looking vine stumps awaiting their winter pruning and with a rather bored Labrador in the back of the car who wanted a walk. No way was I donning wellington boots in the middle of nowhere to tramp across a muddy field when we still had another hour to go ….was I mad to have left home on New Year's Day with a car full of warm clothes and dog food, not forgetting my trusty laptop which was intended to keep me company for the month of January, whilst I wrote the remaining chapter or two and finished my book!

I was actually staying in a different rented house, some 30 miles from the summer property. Clearly a six bedroomed house with six bathrooms was rather excessive for me at this time of the year and I wasn't going to be using the swimming pool, but I experienced sudden pangs of homesickness as I started to spot road signs to places that I had grown to love in the summer. The rain came down harder, the mist became thicker and for a fleeting moment I wondered if I should turn round and return to the utter safety of my English home and husband! I glanced at the milometer, home was 879 miles away, how absurd to even consider such a thought. It will all be fine when I arrive at my destination.

Then as I neared my destination I received a kind text from my landlady. "As it a holiday period and people are not back at work, do make sure that you arrive at the house with plenty of petrol, there are no stations nearby to fill up." That was indeed helpful and I re-routed back towards Bordeaux, to at least be on the N10 and hopefully see petrol stations in abundance. Ten miles down the road, job done and with a full tank once more I headed off in the direction of St Emilion.

I arrived at my village of Puisseguin noting gratefully in the misty conditions that there was a *supermarché,* a pharmacy and a restaurant, this looked promising. But Sat Nav wasn't finished with me, the screen indicated a further mile to go; I arrived in a hamlet of about eight houses, most of them shuttered up and absolutely no sign of life. "You are at your destination" said Sat Nav, but where is the house? I thought, slight panic returning, round the corner and there it was, thank goodness it looked exactly like the photograph. I breathed a huge sigh of relief, at last I had arrived safely for the beginning of my winter adventure.

I remembered the instructions "Pull the outside shutters back and open the kitchen door, the keys will be on the inside of the door." Perfect and I entered into the kitchen; a blast of cold air hit me. Why wasn't the heating on? The owner was in Northern France and I didn't know a soul to call, how would I survive until she returned in four days' time? The house was delightful, very clean and obviously well-equipped but the cold took my breath away. Thank goodness I had bought a dozen large candles with me to add to the evening ambiance, but what else did I have in the car that might help to provide some warmth? I had Harry, our 4-year old black Labrador with me, what role could he take to help out in this predicament? Having always been strict with him about climbing on furniture or on the bed, suddenly the idea of snuggling up to that lovely warm body seemed the only solution! Harry followed me into the house and rather nervously had a sniff round, I could almost see the vapour of his breath as he toured from room to room. In the living room there was a huge fireplace, with what thankfully looked like a wood burning stove, but where was the wood basket filled to the brim in the hearth? On closer inspection this was no wood burner but a fire 'container' obviously fired by pellets but for which there were no instructions nor indeed was there any sign of pellets.

Harry, now sticking to my heels like a child would, followed me upstairs. Yes, a lovely airy bedroom, two large windows thankfully double glazed, with the double bed made up in readiness for a cosy night's sleep in this igloo. In trepidation I turned the duvet back, surely this wasn't a winter tog? We were used to 13.5 togs at home from late September until spring. Thank goodness that whenever possible I always travel with my own bed linen. My 13.5 tog duvet was dragged from the boot of the car up the stairs and the bed was remade, with my own duvet next to me and the original bed linen piled unceremoniously on top. A hot water bottle was filled, inserted in the bed and Harry instructed that despite any rules previously held, he was to jump on the bed immediately I climbed into bed and snuggle up as close to me as he could. The first of the dust sheets that I had also packed to go on the floor for muddy paws was spread over the bed and would be staying there until the heating issues were sorted. I dreaded turning a tap on in case there was no hot water either, but amazingly piping hot water steamed out of all the taps and the shower. I could always thaw out whilst showering and then climb into my new silky (cold) pyjamas, which I had been thrilled to receive as a present on Christmas Day but now I wished had bought my well-worn fleecy Fat Face pyjamas that at least gave a sense of warmth.

So, that was the first night. Harry, obedient as ever jumped on the bed, turned away from me but stretched the full length of his back against mine. In truth I think he was as cold as I was and neither of us dared move an inch all night in case a whisper of cold air from the bedroom came under the duvets.

We had three nights like that, but it is amazing how quickly the body adapts. I had thick sweaters, a couple of *gilets*, my Barbour jacket, gloves, woolly hats, thick socks, Ugg boots, walking boots and wellies. Differing combinations of all of that kept me warm as I ate my meals and worked on my laptop. Luckily I had a pair of fingerless gloves, which allowed me to type and by Monday evening when the owner of the house returned, both Harry and I greeted her quite cheerfully.

"I have recently had to change my housekeeper" she smiling said from outside the front door, "so I hope that everything was fine on your arrival and the house was warm?" " Come in", I said "and see….." Her smile disappeared somewhat as she crossed the icy threshold. It turned out that not only had the new housekeeper not put the heating on, but also she had made up the beds with summer weight linen; suffice to say that once our charming hostess was back in the harness things improved greatly and at speed. When a bottle of champagne and some delicious chocolates were very kindly delivered later that evening, Harry and I were already cosily relaxing in front of the television in our now warm living room.

So now I return to the true purpose of these final chapters and what you are really interested in! What can you do in this area of SW France during the winter months? Although I was taken aback initially by the quietness of the area, there is a real charm to this region even at this time of the year. It took only a few days for me to settle in to the atmosphere of this region again. Most businesses, especially restaurants and clothes shops remain closed for at least the first three weeks of January, then suddenly like a butterfly emerging from a chrysalis everything slowly comes back to life. During this period however there is fervent activity in the vineyards. From early December until March, endless pair of hands tend the vines, removing all the obsolete shoots from last year's grape harvest, and pruning back to a single shoot that will develop and flourish into this year's grape production. There is a further much shorter, secondary shoot that will develop into next year's main growth. It is amazing to think that all of the pruning used to be done by the local women using secateurs; men would on the whole not do this work until secateurs powered by battery packs became available. Lo and behold, now men were happy to get stuck in to the pruning!

Les vignes en hiver

Because I had Harry with me, twice a day we were doing long walks and there were many to choose from. Once it stopped raining and the mist cleared the countryside seemed just as beautiful as in the summer months with dry crisp days that were mainly filled with sunshine. I guess we were lucky with the weather as the ground was still quite soft and muddy from the three weeks of torrential rain that had engulfed the region in December, but after our arrival the ground dried and hardened quickly with the night frosts, even my wellingtons were quickly put aside for my walking boots. There is no doubt that sunshine makes such a difference to how you view your surroundings. Our walks became a real joy. We made friends with several of the local people pruning the vines; the job is painstakingly slow and so each day we had a conversation with the same individuals who had simply moved a few further rows along! These conversations did wonders for my French, as I persistently tried to engage with Eastern European people speaking limited French, students who had come from other areas with different dialects and of course the local farm workers.

However to return to the question of how to occupy yourself in winter, it is a challenge. The tourist offices have limited opening hours at this time of the year, so actually accessing anyone who can advise you is a bit luck of the draw. One day I wanted to post a thick envelope to England, a simple stamp would not suffice as it needed to be weighed, so off I set to a large nearby village where I had seen the *Bureau de Poste* sign whilst driving through a few days earlier. *FERME* was the very definite sign on the door. So onto the nearest town where the post office was open for an hour in the morning and an hour in the afternoon. It was by now nearly midday and lunchtime for all of the locals who would be eating and the post office would certainly not be reopening until 3pm, perhaps I should try again tomorrow? No, I was determined to get this mission accomplished, so now I am heading for Libourne. This town has a large general hospital so surely it would have a post office that was open all day. I eventually found the post office building but parking became the next issue; it was market day and all available spaces had been occupied since dawn. I reached home at 3.00pm, so the task of posting a letter had taken almost five hours. Perhaps this is how the local people occupy themselves each day!

As I was living in a different area of the Gironde in January, the markets were spread around the wider St Emilion region.

Monday -	Castillon-la-Bataille
Tuesday -	Libourne
Wednesday -	Coutras , Creon
Thursday -	Libourne, Branne
Friday -	Libourne , Saint-Medard-de-Guizieres
Saturday -	Libourne, Creon, Saint-Germain-du-Puch, Coutras
Sunday -	Libourne, Saint-Seurin-sur-L'isle, Guitres, Saint-Denis-de-Pile

Markets are a little different in the winter, but I have to admit just as fun. All the winter vegetables look splendid, naturally very fresh, enormous and plentiful. Long queues still exist to get served for the best cuts of meat and luscious looking fish. The cheese stalls are still wonderfully plentiful and at this time of the year each market always has a paella stall which smells very enticing as you wander around, no *vin chaud* stall though which was a bit of a disappointment! The only real difference between the summer and winter markets is that the sundresses are exchanged for winter sweaters, bobble hats, slippers….. and fleecy pyjamas (I bought a lovely cosy pair for 15 euros on my second day here, so cosy in fact that I returned the next day to buy a second pair!).

These markets are always very jolly affairs, with local friends meeting up for the weekly shop, followed by a coffee and pastry. If you stay chatting long enough, the husbands arrive for a beer and then all too quickly its midday, so groups of people move into lunch mode with the delicious aroma of cooked French cheese suddenly filling the air. Some cafes keep their summer chairs and tables outside but apart from the hardy few and the smokers, most people crowd into small steamy cafes and bars for their c*roque monsieur* and green salad. It is interesting that very few people seem to order a c*roque madame*, which is the same as a *croque monsieur* but has a poached egg on the top. I was very relieved that my constant companion Harry was also welcomed into wherever I was drinking coffee or eating; the French do seem to like dogs which was fortunate.

I should add that although I originally planned to drive over to France for January fully intending to spend the month concentrating on undisturbed writing, within a few days of my making the ferry booking it was clear that Mike was keen to join me, and we decided on the last week of January for his arrival by air. Then unsurprisingly plans changed again and I ended up with only 10 days on my own, as Mike hurt his back, couldn't play golf and decided to fly into Bordeaux to support me in my book writing; "I can walk Harry for you then you will have even more time for writing!" The only down side of this extra "visitor" in the house was that my staple diet of bread and cheese and fruit, washed down with an occasional glass of wine flew straight out of the window, suddenly there was a need to cook proper meals on a daily basis with lots of preparation time, oh joy. However true to his word, Mike was a great help, good company and he allowed to me to spend every afternoon and evening working on my book whilst he spent time researching places to visit that could be interesting to my readers!

The morning after Mike arrived there was a loud, insistent knocking at the front door at about 8am, it was *Madame Annie* whom I had met a few days earlier. Smilingly I greeted her in French, *Madame Annie* wasn't smiling. *" Ou est votre chien?"* she demanded. *"Ici,"* I replied. What on earth could the matter be? Harry doesn't bark, he's friendly and a few days ago she appeared to warm to him when we first met in the lane. So in rapid French which thankfully I could follow she described a scene that had occurred late the previous afternoon…her son had left the hen house and the hen garden gate open whilst he popped into the house opposite to have tea with his mother, *Madame Annie*. When he returned later to feed his three hens, one was dead in the hen garden. Did I know anything about this incident she somewhat accusingly demanded, as it clearly wasn't a fox that had attacked the hen but a dog (as she looked angrily around the kitchen for Harry, who had sensibly gone to lie demurely in his bed) Oh no, I thought, how am I going to explain this in French but the best policy is probably complete honesty . "Yes, I do know something about this because I had taken Harry out for a walk about 5pm, and as we walked past the hen garden I noticed that the gate was open and there were lots of feathers on the lane. We carried on with our walk for a mile or so and made a detour through the vineyard to come home; on nearing home Harry and I came across the poor terrified hen, covered in scratches with masses of feathers torn out, but alive." Of course it was easy to put two and two together and on examining the poor hen, I had also thought it couldn't have been a fox as a fox would have taken the hen away and eaten it, so it did look like a dog attack. I couldn't leave the injured hen there in the vineyard, so of course I had picked it up and cradling it in my arms Harry and I walked her back to the hen garden, which by the time we reached the gate had become her heavenly home. Bearing in mind that we are residing in a tiny hamlet surrounded by locals who all know each other and their individual pets. This didn't look good for Harry, although I knew that he had been with me all afternoon in his bed, whilst I had been typing at the table beside him. His "walk" with me had been his first outing of the afternoon and he had been with me all of the time as we walked up the lane.

I could now hear Mike moving around upstairs, clearly wondering what the reasons where for *Madame Annie's* raised voice, oh no please don't let my non-French speaking husband come downstairs and complicate this ghastly situation even more. I was actually quite expecting *Madame Annie's* son to appear around the corner of the house with a shotgun, an eye for an eye and all that, please God, keep Harry in his basket and out of the firing line. Adrenalin thankfully kicked in, my French went up a notch, vocabulary flooded back and despite great sorrow for her son and his hen, I explained quite firmly that we lived on a country estate in England (vast exaggeration but it suited the defence case for my beloved Labrador) Harry was fully trained as a gun dog to retrieve dead birds and then only on command. He had never chased sheep, horses or any live livestock. Sorry as I was about the incident this was not his doing.

Of course *Madame Annie* wanted Harry to be the suspect, but she reluctantly shrugged her shoulders and wishing us a "*bonne journée*" she stood back from the doorstep. Needless to say for the next three weeks, I kept Harry close by me on all of our local walks across the fields just in case a stray bullet headed in our direction.

The worst part of this tale is that that very evening, I had bought a roast chicken to go in the oven for our supper, it wasn't our most enjoyable meal!

Chapter 15:
Interesting places to visit in the winter months

Despite the lack of tourists and the obvious lack of need for places of interest to be open in the January, I still found plenty to do plus there were also places that I wanted to return to. However a bit like the National Trust in England, many places did not open again until Easter, an example of this was the **'Cordeliers Friary and Cloisters' in St Emilion** to which I would have loved to have made a return visit; there were masses of people there in the summer and I was hoping to walk around leisurely and alone! Another example was the **Chateau du Duras** which closes for the month of January. Many of the churches too are closed in the weekdays during the winter months. We had invited our friend Josie to come for the last week in January and make up for her lost week in August. This time she allowed plenty of time to get to the airport and arrived at Bordeaux flying in from Bristol, 10 minutes before my stepson Dan's plane arrived from Geneva. We seriously wondered whether it would be a disappointment for our two guests, with everywhere being so quiet, but not at all as they were soon getting into a pattern of dog walking, having a *plat de jour* at lunchtime, visiting somewhere of interest in the afternoon, another dog walk and it was time to close the curtains, "open the bar", cook supper, light the candles, let the men select and open the wine and commence yet another highly competitive evening of card playing!

Cité du Vin

However, one of the wonderful visits that we did with Josie and Dan in January was to the Cité du Vin, on the quayside in Bordeaux. This amazing project was officially launched in 2016, when Francois Mitterrand inaugurated the building as the largest and most spectacular wine museum in the world. The building welcomed in excess of 480,000 visitors in 2019, and therefore it was a great delight for us to visit in the winter, with no queuing and lots of space to wander around and appreciate all that the museum has to offer. The permanent exhibition laid out spaciously on three floors, comprises numerous thematic modules presented in eight languages, with a plan and headsets to guide you around. The alluring interactive displays are suitable for all ages and are extraordinarily interesting and very thoughtfully presented. Hours passed by… each area offered another treasure …the open plan library was excellent and there were people simply browsing through the multi-cultural wine books, others undertaking wine research projects on their lap tops, others just relaxing in the quiet atmosphere and absorbing the spectacular views. The specifically designed tasting rooms could be booked out for private groups, there were several themed restaurants, a theatre style lecture auditorium and of course the boutique shop was full of tastefully selected wine gadgets, glasses, books and other perfect gifts to take home! But the top two rooms for me were The Belvedere, the wine tasting gallery at the top of the building, followed by The Cellar on the ground floor.

The Belvedere is the highest point in the building and sipping a wine of your choice, you can wander onto the outside circular viewing balcony to appreciate the panoramic views of the river and city buildings. This roof top gallery is dedicated to a "fusion of the senses", with a glass wall that reflects the images of the River Garonne and the city sights, emphasised strongly by the light from thousands of glass bottles that form the ceiling decor. The wooden counter that spreads the length of the room, has a selection of 20 wines reflecting the diversity of wine across the world.

The Cellar in contrast has subdued lighting, a matt black floor and a shiny black ceiling which makes one feel that you are entering a crypt. The cellar holds over 14,000 bottles displayed around the mirrored semi-circular space. These wines represent over 70 countries, with about 300 French wines. People wander around looking at these wonderful examples of wine production and thankfully photography is allowed so wine bottles that one wants to remember can be recorded for later inspection and research. A large selection of these wines can be purchased by the single bottle or as a case.

This innovative wine museum deserves all the credit that it has received. A memorable visit indeed. Would I have enjoyed it as much if I wasn't a wine lover? I think so, looking at the obvious enjoyment and interest on the faces of the visiting young people and children with their parents. There was just so much to do.

Discovering the underground monuments of St Emilion

This was the tour that I put off in the summer because of having to leave Harry in the car in the heat and the size of the crowds. However today on a crisp January morning, Josie and I go to the Tourist Office and book our 11 euro tickets. The tour is in French but the guide is bilingual, so she is happy to answer any complex questions in English. The tour starts with St Emilionus and his hermit's cave. You will recall from chapter 9 that he spent the last 17 years of his life here undertaking several miracles.

There is also a small spring in the cave that Emilianus would have used to baptise local people as they became converted to Christianity. Additionally, beside what would have been a ledge for his bed is a fertility chair that was used for barren woman to sit on, and according to legend within months the barren women would then find themselves pregnant. After visiting the cave where Emilianus lived as a hermit, the tour continued with a visit to the Holy Trinity Chapel above the cave. Then continues on into the catacombs and is followed by a visit to the vast Monolithic Church. It was fascinating to be underground but quite chilly so have a sweater or jacket. The monuments are open all through the year and was a wonderful winter tour with very few visitors around.

CHAPTER 16:
A vineyard tour
at Clos Vieux Rochers in January

This whole area around St Emilion is awash with vineyards and chateaux. There seems little land that separates them with the French having no hedges to divide the fields (or in this case vineyards) as one vineyard literally links to its neighbouring chateau by a small ditch or simply by the change of name on a very expensive looking sign on the land of the adjoining property. As you head into the town of St Emilion you literally pass dozens of Chateaux all with their hectares of vineyards as far as the eye can see. Most of the chateau buildings are large and impressive to look at, beautifully maintained with the sandstone walls gleaming in the soft January sun. Subtle colours seem to be *de rigeur* for the huge shutters that encase every window, light blue, grey and eau de nil green seem to be the favourites. It all looks SO French! Immaculately maintained vineyards with expensively gravelled drives and, adjoining the residential part of the chateau, perfectly kept buildings with large steel doors to keep the *caves* cool for the grape production process and subsequent storage of the barrels.

So having consulted with my sister and her husband who live in this area of France, we decided to visit a vineyard just outside Puisseguin, called Clos Vieux Rochers, an estate owned and run by Rob and Steve, two English guys who bought the property in 2015. Wine making is a complex affair and although my French is passable, it was so much more interesting listening to an English speaking guide!

The whole property has been significantly renovated over the past five years and now includes three one bedroomed *gites,* or guest houses. These properties are situated around a charming courtyard, with ample space for tables and chairs in the summer, from which to admire the views over the countryside and sip a glass or two of their delicious Castillon Cotes de Bordeaux wine. I could quite see myself relaxing under the attractive mulberry tree on the lawn, reading a book and enjoying my *apéritif*.

The tour of the property was fascinating and took about 90 minutes. There was a chilly breeze as we initially stood outside having a lesson on winter pruning, but it is an important part of the whole process to get the pruning correct if the *vignoble* wants to produce a plentiful grape harvest for the coming year. It was noticeable all over the Gironde valley as we toured around that pruning is the main activity for the winter months. Rob estimated that their pruning could be done between the two of them by the end of December if they were lucky with the weather, whereas some of the huge St Emilion vineyards could continue with their pruning tasks until March before the work was complete.

The tour progressed into the building where the grapes are delivered once harvesting has begun, and Rob continued to explain each cycle of the wine making process. It is a tough life and some of the tasks have to be undertaken to precision or the wine is ruined. No time to feel ill or wanting a day off! The tour finished, we moved into the tasting room to sample the red wine and rosé that the guys specialise in. We sampled two years, 2017 and 2016, both delicious although personally I preferred the 2016, full of fruity flavour and on the inhalation of the bouquet before tasting, the vanilla and blackberry flavours were distinctive. Interestingly all of the previous year's wine had been sold, not surprising as 2015 was deemed to be an excellent year for the *vignobles*.

I should add that there is a small charge for the tour of the estate and to hear Rob's interesting and humorous anecdotes about their lives in producing wine in France, but that is waived or discounted if purchases of the wine are made. Our dilemma was estimating how many cases we could safely pack into the car to take back to England.

https://www.closvieuxrochers.com

CHAPTER 17:
Eating out in Winter

Many of the local restaurants are closed in January. The restaurant owners seem to decide for themselves for how long they remain closed and the notices on the door vary from "opening again on 5th January" to "closing for the month of January" or in one restaurant window I saw a sign saying "opening again on the 1st March". Many of the restauranteurs and their families will make the most of this winter lull to refresh themselves and fit in some weeks of relaxing skiing in the Alps.

The Old Bookshop in Duras
This is a coffee shop but with a real difference. It feels so healthy to enter this warm and cosy cafe off the Market Square in Duras. Relaxing, colourful sofas to sink into, healthy options on the menu and run by a charming French *Madame* who makes all of her own cakes, pastries and snacks, both sweet and savoury.

The Caffe Cuisine in Branne
This was one of those restaurants that had a look of a junk shop about it as we approached. The outside courtyard was devoid anything that looked in the slightest bit welcoming. There was a sign that said the restaurant was open but that was it. No shrubs in pots, no twinkling lights, the umbrellas stacked in a corner and all of the tables and chairs piled up on top of each other. The arched doorway was an attractive feature but other than that…so we walked across the courtyard with some trepidation even though we had booked a table for four of us for lunch. In we walked at 12.30pm and goodness me how our hearts lifted. The front room, as that was what it looked like, was full except for one table laid for four people in the corner. People laughing,

sipping their wine and obviously enjoying their meal, the most delicious smells wafting through from the kitchens confirmed that whatever people were eating was good! There weren't two chairs the same, every table was of a different design, mostly wooden but round, square and oblong, the furniture was completely understated and had clearly come from the local *brocantes* and *antiquities*. It just looked like whatever would fit into this room had been selected! Without any qualms whatsoever we headed to the remaining table in the corner. *"Oh non Madame, vous avez une reservation n'est ce* pas?" We all turned to see the *Madame* in charge heading across the room, *"Vous etes dans la salle a manger"*… "I didn't know there was another room", my sister whispered; we dutifully left our corner and followed Madame into an utterly charming, much larger dining room with just as much clutter and chaos as far as the furnishings were concerned but a lovely old fashioned wood burner in the corner giving off just the right amount of heat, and a traditional heavy wooden mahogany bar so reminiscent of French bars and restaurants in the past, decked with sparkling wine glasses, bottles of wine, baskets of bread and a pile of well ironed white linen napkins. We were shown to a table next to the bar; looking around us the whole restaurant was full and it was only 12.40pm! This looked like a great find and we couldn't wait to see what was on the menu. Everyone was eating the *plat du jour* at 18 euros for three courses, no need to ponder further as the decision was made. After an *apéritif* of a crisp dry wine, the first course of *soup de poisson* arrived with julienne strips of leeks and other delicious vegetables amongst the broth. Just scrummy and washed down with another glass of this delicious white wine. It is worth noting that in France, nobody asks whether you want a small, medium or large glass of wine, you are simply served a modest amount that comes to where the bowl of the glass begins to widen. As I discussed in an earlier chapter the type and shape of the wine glass is important. The second course was just as mouth-watering, comprised of pulled veal, so tender that it fell apart as you touched it with your fork, beautifully cooked vegetables, a carrot puree and a "smearing" of truffle oil puree spread across one side of the plate. It was a whitish colour and my sister who hadn't got her glasses with her thought it was a ceramic decoration that was part of the plate design and traced round it delicately with her index finger! Those plates were left clean too and then the choice was around the dessert, three *chocolate pastries à Paris* and *à Baba au Rhum*. All melted in your mouth and then a wonderful coffee to complete our lunch. Just over 100 euros for four of us to have a feast that was very memorable, leisurely and ensured that none of us needed further food that day. I will never understand how the French women stay so slim...

Le Bistro de Gare, Puisseguin

I ate here in our village on my second night when I was still suffering from hypothermia from the lack of heating. Harry was welcomed in too and dutifully lay beside my chair. This meal was most enjoyable and I started with an unusual first course of poached egg resting on a bed of julienne vegetable strips and a very delicious *jus*. It was almost like French onion soup but with a poached egg added. This was followed by a delicious piece of cod stuffed with prawns and covered with a rich sauce. I had one glass of Chateau du Môle recommended by the waiter, from one of the local vineyards in Puisseguin which was known for producing this wonderfully smooth Cabernet Sauvignon. It was a very good meal and the staff were kind and attentive to both Harry and I, however after scrutinising the bill any return meals will be enjoyed at lunchtime with the amazingly good value *plat du jour*!

L'Ardoise in Pessac-sur-Dordogne

It becomes rather repetitive after a while extolling the virtue of every restaurant we visit, but it IS very unlucky to have a disappointing meal in this region of France. The produce is always very fresh and when you see what is on display in the daily markets it is unsurprising that the food that is presented on your plate is consistently of a high standard. I need to point out though that although you see the French children tucking into these meals with great gusto and to my mind, sophistication, I am not sure how many English youngsters I would expect to see selecting *huitres and Coquille St Jacques* off a menu when there was the choice of a roast chicken and chips on offer!

L'Ardoise in Pessac is a lovely example of a fine dining restaurant for a special night out. We were invited there as a treat and the food was indeed memorable starting with the *amusée bouche,* which comes as a gift from the Chef at the start of the meal to stimulate your taste buds... It does sound very pretentious but in fact it is a way of commencing the evening by stimulating your taste buds for what is to come; this is then followed by the starters, the main courses and desserts. More and more frequently if we were in a group eating out, we would order two or three desserts which we then shared between us.

Cave du Vins St-Genes-de-Castillon

We arrived at midday, were shown to our lunch table and then offered a wine list. Did we want to order a specific bottle of wine for lunch, "no" we explained, "we don't know the Cote de Castillon wines well, and we would like to sample one or two wines from the local grapes if we may?" Most of the Côtes de Castillon are predominately Merlot, which wasn't particularly to my taste, but then we tasted some wine which also contained Cabernet Sauvignon; it altered the taste completely and for me became quite delicious. A Chateau de Monsegur was very memorable although this is 75% Merlot. One of the local wines, a mixture of Malbec and Cabinet Sauvignon, with no Merlot was deliciously refreshing, a little like a white wine would be, with a lovely floral fragrance emerging from the glass, a wine that would be very pleasant to drink on its own without food accompaniments . This particular wine turned out to be a Chateau Beynat, of which there are four Castillon varieties and the price of this bottle was amazingly good value at 4.50 euros. We eventually opted for a bottle of Chateau de Monsegur to accompany our lunch which was another amazing *plat du jour*. Creamy and deliciously smooth cauliflower soup, followed by cod and cous cous with a dish of varied beautifully presented vegetables. Then a white chocolate pannacotta with crumbled ginger biscuit on the top, a *grand creme cafe* to finish and a discussion in the car of how we were going to rid ourselves, once more, of our calories.

L' Atelier de Candale: St Emilion (again ….)

I have to finish this culinary section with my very favourite restaurant situated on the hillside on the outskirts of St Emilion overlooking the endless vineyards down towards the Dordogne River in the far distance. In the summer there is a large terrace with umbrellas for shade and beautifully laid tables, simply inviting you to come in and eat! However unless you book it is unlikely there will be free table on the terrace. In January we ate inside in the understated but charmingly decorated dining room. This lunch was our treat from Josie and therefore we really hoped that the restaurant and its *chef* would not disappoint. No chance of that and we once again gloried in the delights of beautifully cooked and imaginatively presented regional dishes. We savoured a bottle of St Emilion Grand Cru as we languished over our last lunch. What a wonderful time we had had in this charming area of France once again.

So the book is complete and I hope you have enjoyed some of my adventures. I continue my love affair with France and only hope that now the UK has left the European Union and when Covid 19 travel restrictions have been finally lifted that it will remain as easy to visit France as it has always been.

Au revoir mes amis, merci beaucoup et a bientôt.

Thanks and Acknowledgements

To my husband Mike for his continual and loving support.

To Louise Wakeford for her constant encouragement and for creating the beautiful illustrations.

To Keith Thornborough for his advice on research sources and advising me on the content.

To my dear friend Josie Whitfield for her time and diligence in proof reading the manuscript.

To Laura Wakeford and Lucy Slater for their encouragement and interest in the book.

To all of the following family and friends who I suspect initially felt quite sceptical about this project, particularly the time commitment involved for me to complete the book, but who have been constant in their enthusiasm and good wishes. I thank them all. Sarah and Chris Jordan, Rob and Jude Walker, Alex Jordan, Tom Slater, Sally Noy Scott, Pam Paine, Ann Marcer, Helen Tworkowski, Renata Hopkins, Irene Hicks, Tom Wakeford, George Walker, Dan Jefferies, Kate Jefferies, Mike Cummings, Sue Powne, Anita Townsend, Gerald and Sheila Cramp, Richard and Linda Dawson, Lizzie and Nick Barrett, Humphrey and Linda Wheeler, Pete and Di Kersey, Sharon Christian and Karine Devilder.

Most importantly to Bob Fowke from YouCaxton Publications and his excellent team who have assisted me in publishing this book. This would have impossible to do without their professional expertise and advice.

- and a big hug to Harry, for his loyalty and companionship on this journey together.

Suggested further reading for your interest

History of France - Lucien Bely: published by Éditions Gisserot, Paris France, 2001.

Searching for family and traditions at the French table - Carole Bumpus: published by She Writes Press, Canada, 2019,
(ISBN 978-1-63152-549-0).

One more croissant for the road - Felicity Cloake: published by Harper Collins UK, 2019, (ISBN 978-00-0-830493-5).

Grape expectations - Caro Feely: published by Summersdale Publishers, Chichester, 2012, (ISBN 978-1-84953-257-0)

Saving our skins - Caro Feely: published by Summersdale Publishers, Chichester, 2014 (ISBN 978-1-84953-609-7).

Glass half full - Caro Feely: published by Summersdale Publishers, Chichester, 2017, (ISBN 978-1-84953-991-3).

France, an amazingly short history - Bob Fowke: published by Travelbrief Publications, Shrewsbury, 2004,
(ISBN 0-9548351-1-5).

Let's eat France - Francois-Regis Gaudry: published by Artisan Books, New York, 2018, (ISBN 978-1-57965-876-2).

My four seasons in France - Janine Marsh: published by Michael O'Mara Books, London, 2020, (ISBN 978-1-78929-047-9).

The Glitch - Philip Oglivy: published by Canapé Publishing, UK, 2019, (ISBN 978-1-69115878-2).

Index

About the Author

Annie Jefferies lives in Devon with her husband, Mike and black Labrador, Harry. Annie is a Chartered Physiotherapist who retired 10 years ago and this is her first book. Her interests are varied and include walking on Dartmoor, learning Spanish, music, sports, cooking, travelling with family and friends and supporting the Diocese of Exeter as a member of the laity.

BV - #0028 - 250820 - C11 - 203/133/6 - PB - 9781913425340